World War One

SHEFFIELD CARES FOR THE WOUNDED

A story of dedication and bravery

Disclaimer

Every effort has been made to ensure the accuracy of the information contained in this publication. However, the content of this book is intended to be of general guidance and furthermore, no responsibility can be accepted by the authors, editor or publishers for any errors or omissions contained therein.

World War One

SHEFFIELD CARES FOR THE WOUNDED

A story of dedication and bravery

ISBN: 978-0-9568366-7-0

Edited by Dr. Derek R. Cullen

Printed by
J W Northend Limited
Sheffield

Contents

Introduction

A year ago, a friend, Mrs Susan Murray, showed me a silver salver that had been given to her father-in-law, Dr Charles Graham Murray, on the occasion of his marriage, by members of the 3rd West Riding Field Ambulance. It was inscribed with the signatures of medical colleagues, one of whom, Ernest Finch, I immediately recognised as a very famous figure in the history of the Sheffield University Medical School. What therefore was the Field Ambulance and who were the people who had signed their names on this wedding present? The answers to these questions revealed a fascinating story of dedication and bravery of volunteer doctors, orderlies, nurses and stretcher bearers of the Territorial Army who formed the Ambulance and cared for the wounded on the battlefields of France and Flanders in the Great War. Large numbers of wounded and sick soldiers also returned from the battlefields to this country and in Sheffield these were cared for by volunteer doctors and nurses of the 3rd Northern General Hospital in the city's hospitals, halls, schools and even cricket pavilions, where more than 70,000 soldiers were treated throughout the war.

The soldiers of the Field Ambulance also produced a trench journal called 'The Lead Swinger' with articles, poems, sketches and cartoons, the contributors using a 'nom de plume' or as they said a 'nom de guerre'. The contents of this journal give an important insight into their determination to bring a modicum of normality into the lulls between the carnage of the battles. I have taken the liberty of incorporating some of the contents of this journal into the book's text to illustrate this spirit.

It was decided by the Faculty of Medicine that in this centenary year of the beginning of the Great War we should hold an exhibition, complemented by this book, telling this story.

Derek Cullen

Acknowledgements

I would like to thank all those who have contributed to this book which accompanies the exhibition and for the painstaking research necessary to verify the accuracy of its contents. In particular I would like to thank Drs. James Burton, Michael Collins, and John Rochester for their enthusiastic support for the project. Susan Bridgeford, Catherine Davison and Victoria Hattersley of Sheffield University Medical School have very ably managed the administrative aspects, which not perhaps surprisingly have been more considerable than anticipated. I would also like to acknowledge the help and advice of Dr. Lynne Fox, the Heritage Officer of Sheffield University and Ian Palmer, the Leader of the IT support team of the Faculty of Medicine, Dentistry and Health. Miles Stevenson and Louise Shaw from the University of Sheffield's Development, Alumni Relations and Events Office have been invaluable for their encouragement and help in seeking financial support. We are also very grateful to Sheffield University Medical School, Sheffield Town Trust, Sheffield Grammar School Exhibition Foundation, Westfield Health, Sheffield University Alumni Association and the Heritage Lottery Fund for their generous funding of this project

The contributors are particularly grateful to the invaluable help provided by the Sheffield University Library and Special Collections, Sheffield Archives and Local Studies Library, Tyne and Wear Archives and Museums, the National Archives, the Imperial War Museum, the Army Medical Services Museum, the Red Cross Museum, the National Railway Museum, the Liddle Collection in the University of Leeds, the National Library of Scotland and the Daily Mail Archives. Every effort has been made to obtain permission to publish photographs.

A most encouraging aspect of this project has been the great interest displayed by members of the public, not only locally, but from throughout the country. It has been quite amazing how descendants of the members of the Ambulance have responded to our publicity in newspapers and the University Alumni website. Their generosity in donating very precious family archives and artefacts has been very touching and very much in keeping with the spirit of their ancestors who volunteered to serve their country so long ago.

Finally I would like to thank Professor Tony Weetman, Pro-Vice Chancellor of the University of Sheffield Faculty of Medicine, Dentistry and Health, for responding so enthusiastically to the proposal to stage this exhibition and for his continuing support. It will serve to document and commemorate a little known aspect of the history of the Medical Profession in Sheffield.

Derek Cullen

Foreword

It is a real pleasure to write the Foreword to this comprehensive volume which accompanies the Faculty's exhibition. Assembled by Dr. Derek Cullen, it describes vividly and poignantly the contribution that clinical colleagues from Sheffield made to the huge national effort in response to the outbreak of the First World War. This year sees, of course, the centenary of the declaration of that war, and much ink has already been expended on the complex political situation that led up to the war, and the military engagements that then ensued. However, for me, and I suspect most people, what really resonates is the forgotten voice, the echo of someone serving in the conflict who could well have been you or me. What was their experience, what did they see and feel?

This exhibition and book allows us to understand what it was like for those who found themselves exposed to these most extreme of circumstances, to see how they innovated and to appreciate how clinical care was forced to advance as the carnage took its toll. Reading these superbly written vignettes, it's impossible not to imagine how one would have felt and reacted if caught up in these momentous events – and that is real history. I am also sure that the spirit which comes across in these pages reflects the reaction to the war that all Sheffielders would have had, no matter what their occupation. I am extremely grateful to everyone who has contributed to this project, but especially to Derek Cullen, who has ensured that we have a fitting and lasting memento of a significant part of our city's contribution in this 100th anniversary year.

Tony Weetman

Sir Arthur Hall – Professor of Medicine and Pro-Vice Chancellor, Faculty of Medicine, Dentistry and Health

Contributors

Rodney Amos, *Consultant Rheumatologist Emeritus, Royal Hallamshire Hospital, Sheffield.*

David Baldwin, *Retired Hospital Manager, Royal Hallamshire Hospital, Sheffield.*

Denise Thwaites Bee, *Research Fellow in Medical Education, University of Sheffield Medical School.*

Norman Briffa, *Consultant Cardiovascular Surgeon, Northern General Hospital, Sheffield.*

James Burton, *Formerly Director, University Health Service, University of Sheffield.*

Michael Collins, *Consultant Radiologist Emeritus, Royal Hallamshire Hospital, Sheffield.*

Miles Connell, *Rtd., Lloyd's Insurance Broker.*

Derek Cullen, *Consultant Physician Emeritus, Royal Hallamshire Hospital, Sheffield.*

Howard David, *Prothesist, Blanchford and Sons Ltd., Northern General Hospital, Sheffield.*

Sheila Duncan, *Emeritus Reader in Obstetrics and Gynaecology, University of Sheffield.*

Giles Fletcher, *Submarine Nuclear, Electrical and Weapon Engineer Officer.*

Patricia and Trevor Hall, *Retired.*

Barry Hancock, *Emeritus Professor of Oncology, University of Sheffield.*

Paula Hancock, *Emeritus Senior Nursing Lecturer, University of Sheffield.*

Rory Herbert, *Company Secretary, Note Harbour Ltd.*

Paul Ince, *Professor of Neuropathology, University of Sheffield.*

Virge James, *Consultant Haematologist Emeritus, National Blood Service.*

John Mackinnon, *Consultant Cardiologist Emeritus, Birmingham.*

Bob Moore, *Professor of 20th Century European History, University of Sheffield.*

Adrian Padfield, *Consultant Anaesthetist Emeritus, Royal Hallamshire Hospital, Sheffield.*

Judy Redman, *Principal Lecturer, Sheffield Hallam University.*

Tom Scotland, *Consultant Orthopaedic Surgeon Emeritus, Grampian Health Board.*

Geoffrey Travis, *Magistrate.*

Peter Warr, *Emeritus Professor of Psychology, University of Sheffield.*

Eric Wood, *Butchers' Sundriesman, Retired.*

Accident or design?
The origins of the Great War

The treaty signed at Versailles on 28th June 1919 that formally ended the Great War included Article 231, subsequently referred to as the 'war guilt' clause. This stipulated that Germany and her allies took responsibility 'for causing all the loss and damage' during the conflict. Coming at the beginning of the sections of the treaty dealing with reparations, its purpose in justifying the financial and territorial demands was clear, but the wider implication was that Germany had been primarily responsible for the war itself. This went against German perceptions that they had been fighting a defensive war and prompted subsequent attempts by successive German governments and by historians to question exactly how this most destructive of all conflicts came about. In trying to explain the relationship between the multitude of factors involved in both the extent and the timing of the conflict, the historian James Joll posited the idea of concentric circles radiating out from the 'July crisis' of 1914 to include the preceding arms race, imperialist and economic rivalries and the all-important domestic contexts to the formation of foreign policy by all the Great Powers of Europe.

There is no doubt that heightened nationalist sentiment played a major role in many countries; seen as a unifying force in Imperial Germany while creating problems in the multi-ethnic and polyglot Austro-Hungarian Empire. Indeed, it had been Slav nationalism and Austrian responses that had been responsible for two small-scale wars between Austria and Serbia in 1912 and 1913, although neither of these had escalated into a pan-European conflict. German nationalism had been fostered to create political alliances in a newly united country, but one that was divided economically between the interests of agrarians and industry, confessionally between Lutherans and Roman Catholics, and politically between Conservatism, Liberalism and Social Democracy. Having begun by building an anti-Catholic political consensus in the 1870s, Chancellor Otto von Bismarck and his successors chose to isolate the increasing threat of organised social democracy and thus unite otherwise disparate and sometimes conflicting economic and political interests. In order to cement this, there was an increasing focus on national prestige and on expansion.

In 1890, Bismarck, undoubtedly the most able statesman of his day, retired from government. The architect of German unification in 1871, he had also built a series of international treaties to guarantee the country's long-term security. The keystone of this was the Dual Alliance with Austria Hungary in 1879, designed to provide a collective defence against aggression from Imperial Russia. This was augmented in 1882 by a similar treaty with Italy which was largely directed against France. Defeat in the war of 1870-1 meant that successive governments in Paris had to confront the threat of a rapidly industrialising and unified Germany on their Eastern border.

1

Mutual mistrust generated an arms race and a feeling that France also needed to protect itself through international alliances. Of the two remaining Great Powers, any Anglo-French understanding would have to overturn at least 600 years of animosity and there was little common ground between a democratic republican France and an Tsarist autocracy in Russia. While Bismarck had successfully kept France isolated, his successors were less adept – allowing previous treaties with Moscow to lapse. In 1894, in pursuit of greater security, France and Russia signed a defensive military alliance. The division of the Great Powers into two opposing power blocs was reinforced in 1903-4 when Britain negotiated an *entente cordiale* with France, ostensibly only to settle outstanding colonial conflicts, and then in 1907 with an Anglo-Russian convention which resolved the two powers' rivalries in Asia. Although by no means a comprehensive political or military alliance, this so-called triple entente effectively ended Britain's long-term policy of avoiding European commitments. Isolation had served Britain well during the nineteenth century but the growth of Germany, increasing colonial rivalries and the problems of imperial security highlighted by the Boer War all served to force London to rethink its position.

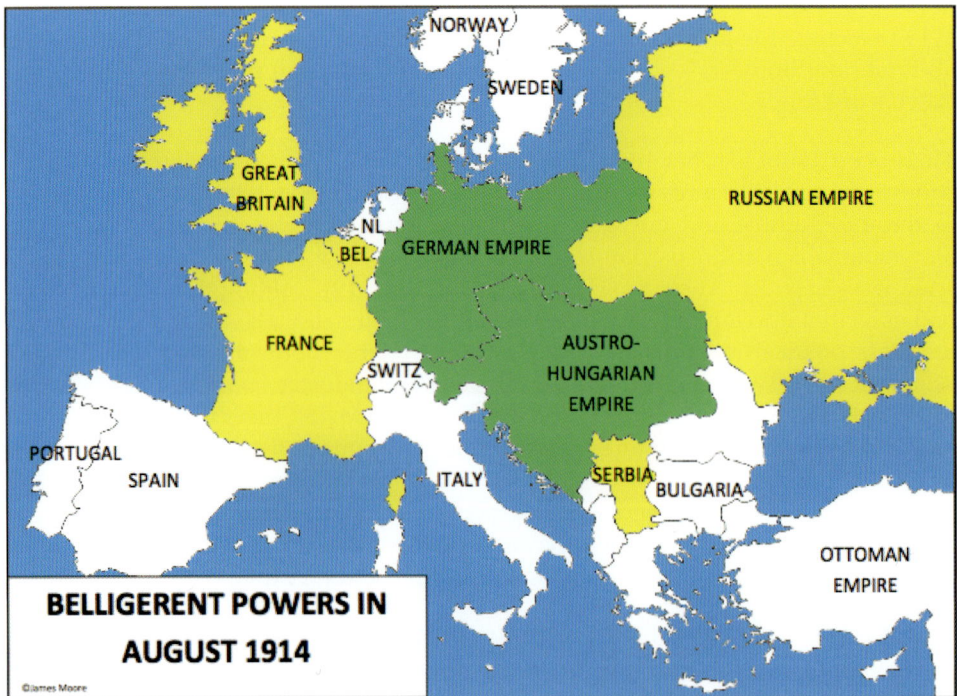

BELLIGERENT POWERS IN AUGUST 1914

While Bismarck had been an impartial host of the 1884-5 Berlin Conference which had effectively divided up the African continent among Europe's imperial states, his successors after 1890 increasingly spoke of Germany also having its 'place in the sun', a tendency reinforced by the activities of adventurers such as Adolf Lüderitz in South West Africa and Carl Peters in East Africa. In tandem with this overseas expansion came demands for a fleet to protect newly-won imperial territories. This served a dual purpose of providing a focus for nationalist sentiment and also a justification for massive state expenditure in the country's heavy industries. These had been hard-hit by foreign tariff barriers which had been created in response to Berlin's continuing commitment to protecting German agriculture (and therefore the fortunes of its Junker ruling class). While German territorial ambitions could probably be 'managed' by the other powers, their naval building programme was to bring direct conflict with the British naval supremacy at the beginning of the twentieth century. With the enthusiastic backing of Kaiser Wilhelm II, Rear-Admiral Alfred von Tirpitz began an expansion programme from 1897 onwards. This led to an arms race to build ever faster and better armed battleships, culminating in what became known as the dreadnought campaign. This race for technical superiority was given added importance by the defeat of the Russian Imperial fleet by the Japanese at the battle of Tsushima in May 1905. The superior guns of the Japanese ships allowed them to stand off the Russians and inflict murderous damage on their hapless enemies.

While there is no doubt that international tensions had been growing in the first decade of the twentieth century; tensions that had spawned an arms race among the major powers and perhaps also an expectation in the minds of the public that there would be a war sooner or later, it does not explain why the murder of the Archduke Franz Ferdinand, the heir to the Habsburg Empire, by the Bosnian Serbian nationalist, Gavril Princip in July 1914 precipitated a general European war within a matter of five weeks. While the assassination was a potentially serious diplomatic incident between Austria and Serbia, there was no inevitability that large-scale war would ensue. The Austrians blamed Serbian support for Slav nationalism within the Habsburg lands and there was strong pressure in Vienna for military action. The danger was that this would provoke Serbia's ally Russia into offering support, and thus Emperor Franz-Jozef wrote personally to Kaiser Wilhelm asking for German backing for their proposed action against the Serbs. Wilhelm's reply, the so-called 'blank cheque' offered unconditional German support even if Russia became involved. With this reassurance, the Austrians drafted an ultimatum to Serbia – the contents of which were both deliberately humiliating and a direct attack on Serbian sovereignty. Its delivery was delayed by more than a week to allow more time for the harvest to be gathered and to avoid it arriving during a French state visit to Russia, but when finally presented in Belgrade on the afternoon of 23rd July it came with a 48 hour deadline for compliance. With several members of government away from the capital, those still there played for time and actually agreed to all but one of the Austrian demands. This was nonetheless deemed unsatisfactory by the Habsburg government, suggesting that it was exactly the outcome it had hoped for. It had been assumed that German backing for Austria would act as a deterrent to Russian involvement, but this was soon exposed as illusory, with the Russian Foreign Minister accusing the Austrians of 'setting Europe afire'. British attempts at mediation in an effort to limit hostilities foundered on the unwillingness of the

Germans to participate, again suggesting that the Kaiser and his government were driving Austrian intransigence.

French attitudes in this crucial period were complicated by the fact that the President and Prime Minister were returning from Russia by sea and received only garbled reports of what was happening via an imperfect telegraph system. Indecision by government ministers still in Paris convinced the Germans and Austrians that France would not honour its treaty obligations to Russia in the event of war, whereas the French ambassador in St. Petersburg was conveying exactly the opposite message to the Russians. Only when her leaders arrived back in France on 29th July was there a more robust response although some military preparations had been made by the Armed Forces. By this time, the Austrians had declared war on Serbia and bombarded Belgrade. Subsequent attempts at negotiation were hampered by indecision in all the major capitals of Europe as the full magnitude of the crisis unfolded and matters were increasingly dictated by perceived military imperatives. Nowhere was this more evident than in the Russian general mobilisation of 30th July made essential by the knowledge that it would take longer to get the Tsarist armies into the field than their potential enemies. This allowed the German and Austrian governments to portray their subsequent general mobilisations as defensive measures. With France committed to its Russian ally, a general European war was only days away and allowed for the full implementation of the German Schlieffen Plan that involved an immediate attack on France to remove her as a threat before a more sustained and inevitably longer campaign against Russia.

The British involvement in the deepening crisis, and specifically the actions of Foreign Secretary, Sir Edward Grey, have come under close scrutiny and evoked some criticism. The public and even government perception of the treaties and diplomatic understandings that linked Britain with France and separately with Russia were widely regarded as sufficiently loose to allow for some interpretation and British involvement in the looming conflict in July 1914 was by no means a foregone conclusion. In the last days of July, Grey had attempted to broker a settlement using his good offices with the Russians while trusting Berlin's ability to hold an increasingly belligerent Austria in check. Russian mobilisation on 30th July effectively ended any hopes that war in Eastern Europe could be avoided altogether, but there was still the chance that Germany and France could be kept out of the conflict, in spite of their respective alliance commitments. His miscalculation in this strategy stemmed from an assumption that Germany and its Kaiser would want to avoid a war. It has also been argued that by refusing to commit Britain wholeheartedly to the Triple Entente and by continuing to negotiate, Grey actually encouraged Berlin to think that Britain would remain neutral and thus allowed the Germans to think they had a free hand. Grey's prevarication may have stemmed from a belief in the power of negotiation or that by keeping British intentions secret it would give both sides pause for thought, but he was also aware that the Cabinet itself was split and that some members would not support a war under any circumstances.

Even when both Germany and France mobilised on 1st August, the British government had made no firm decisions. A Cabinet meeting on the afternoon of 2nd August had accepted that a secret 'exchange of letters' between Britain and France in 1912 that divided responsibility for naval security between the two powers obliged Britain to intervene if a German fleet came into the Channel or the North Sea, but there was no outright military commitment to France. In some respects, the Asquith Cabinet was saved from having to justify war on the basis of a treaty about whose terms even some government ministers were unaware by the German plans for an attack on France. German demands for free passage for their troops through neutral Belgium as part of the Schlieffen Plan brought into play the international guarantee of that country's neutrality that had existed since 1839. Thus when the Belgians mounted an armed resistance against German incursions on their territory, Britain had no real choice but to send an ultimatum to Berlin demanding the immediate honouring of Belgian neutrality. When the ultimatum expired at midnight on 4th August, Britain joined the war that would last for more than four years, prompting unforeseeable irreversible political, social and economic changes across Europe and costing the lives of many millions of people.

Bob Moore

The 3rd West Riding Field Ambulance

The history of field ambulances goes back to the Crusades when the Knights of St. John or as we know them today, the Knights of Malta, treated the wounded of both sides of a battle removing them from the battlefield for further care. The concept of army field hospitals from which medical attendants could give aid to the wounded and bring them back on stretchers or carts was first developed by Baron Dominique Larrey, Napoleon's Surgeon in Chief, in the late 18th century and refined in the American Civil War (1861-65) when each regiment with its own medical staff manned a regimental aid post near to the front line giving immediate care to the wounded. The American Surgeon, General William A. Hammond, also improved the transport of the wounded away from the battlefield designing the first purpose built ambulance. Despite such welcome improvements, in the care of the wounded, more soldiers died from disease than wounds. In the Crimean War (1854-56) five times as many men died from diseases such as cholera, typhoid fever and typhus than from wounds and even in the Boer War (1899-1902), typhoid fever killed more British troops than enemy action.

The problem was complicated by the fact that doctors were poorly paid and did not have any military rank so that they were not attracted to Army service which as a result was severely undermanned. Furthermore, doctors were not involved in the provision of health for soldiers, although the work of Dr. James Barry and Florence Nightingale in the Crimean War improving sanitation for soldiers with the provision of clean drinking water and adequate disposal of sewage had demonstrated a fall in the death rates from infectious disease. Despite opposition from the War Office, the status of doctors in the Army was gradually improved by the formation of the Royal Army Medical Corps (RAMC) in 1898 and by the enlightened and far reaching reforms of the British Army brought in by Sir Richard later Lord Haldane, the Secretary of State for War from 1906 to 1912. These created an Expeditionary Force of regular soldiers to be used as an interventional force in times of crisis abroad supported by a Territorial Force of volunteers for home defence and the establishment of Officer Training Corps in universities and public schools to ensure a supply of officers to the Army in wartime. Practising doctors and medical students were trained in these forces and at the same time the benefits of improved sanitation and inoculation against typhoid on the health of the Army led to the recognition of the importance of medical opinion in the regulation of the nation's armed services.

The medical and sanitary services for the new Territorial forces were to be provided by volunteer doctors joining the RAMC and forming a field ambulance. In Sheffield, this was raised in 1908 at the Sheffield Corn Exchange becoming known as the 1/3 West Riding Field Ambulance (3rd WRFA) and the first Commanding Officer was

Lt. Col. T. Stewart Adair. With growth of the unit they moved to premises at 2 Gell Street. After five years, Lt. Col. Adair left the unit and was replaced for a short time by Major F. A. Hadley who was a surgeon at the Royal Infirmary and who emigrated to Australia in 1912 subsequently becoming a founder of the Royal Australian College of Surgeons. He was replaced in 1913 by Lt. Col. John W. Stokes who was a surgeon living in Crookes, Sheffield.

When mobilised, a field ambulance was attached to an infantry brigade i.e. 4,000 troops. Its personnel consisted of 9 Medical Officers and 1 Dental Officer, a Chaplain and Other Ranks which included nursing orderlies, stretcher bearers, clerks, cooks etc. to a total of 241 men and it carried reserve field dressings to cope with at least 2,000 casualties. In the early stages of the war the field ambulance transport would be with horse drawn wagons and later by motor ambulances. In the event of a major action all the field ambulances of a division i.e. three brigades might be grouped together.

3rd WRFA arriving in France in April 1915

When war was declared on 4th August, 1914, the 3rd WRFA were camped at Whitby undergoing its annual summer camp training. They immediately returned to Sheffield and mobilised fully, then they trained in Lincolnshire before they embarked for France several months later. It is recorded in Major Mackinnon's diary that in October 1914 they spent two weeks in Sandbeck Park, Maltby, during which Major Mackinnon, who was second in command, received his anti-typhoid vaccination, the first one in the arm and the second 10 days later in the chest. On 7th April, 1915, they received news that they were shortly due to embark for France and during the next few days they had '3 cases of appendicitis operated on by Finch' (Ernest Finch was to become Professor of Surgery at Sheffield Royal Infirmary). On the 15th April they left Gainsborough by train for Southampton where they embarked on the S.S. Golden Eagle and S.S. Southampton for France and after a smooth passage arrived in Le Havre on the 16th April. Then, having had some difficulty boarding their trucks and wagons, they left by train via Abbeyville, St. Omer, Hazlebrouchk, to Merville, where they arrived on 18th April subsequently marching to billets on a farm east of Estaires on the road to Dolieu. Here they had their first experience of war *seeing light flares with guns going intermittently and aeroplanes moving overhead at frequent intervals* and formed their first advanced dressing station.

The Western Front from the Sea to Arras © Daily Mail Archives

A field ambulance was an independent mobile medical unit and in order to understand its function it is necessary to describe how casualties were evacuated from the field of battle. They would first be taken to a regimental aid post (RAP) close to the frontline by stretcher bearers where they would be seen by the battalion medical officer and his orderlies. They would perform basic first aid such as ensuring that wounds were adequately dressed and shock would be treated with warm dry blankets and either rectal or subcutaneous fluids (it would be 1917 before stored blood for blood transfusion would be available) and fractured femurs would be properly

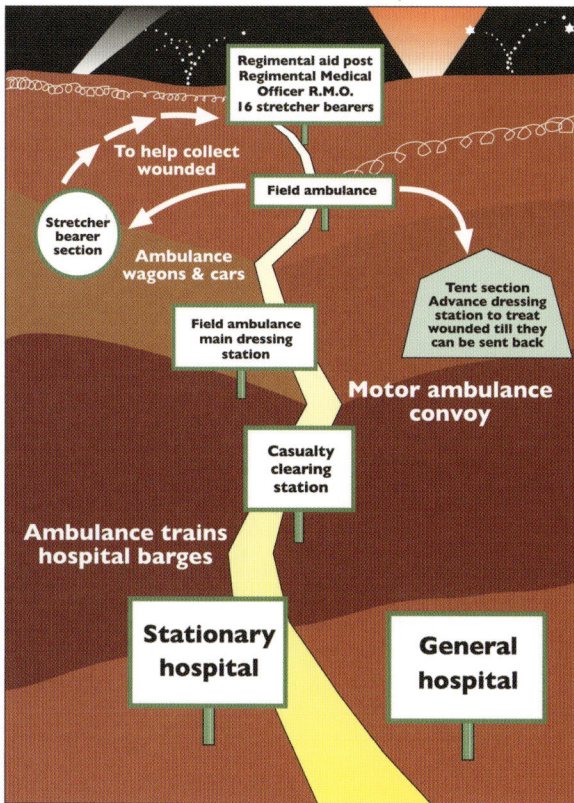

Evacuation Route for the wounded © Tom Scotland

splinted with a Thomas Splint. The wounded would then be transported by the stretcher bearers of the field ambulance to the advanced dressing station (ADS) whose function was to triage the wounded into three categories. The lightly wounded were treated and sent to the Main Dressing Station (MDS) where a decision was taken as to whether they could return to the front line. The severely wounded would be sent back to the nearest casualty clearing station (CCS) which was usually out of range of artillery shelling where they would receive specialist treatment, some of these specialising in certain types of wound. Major surgery would not be performed at the ADS except for amputations to stop major bleeding but would be performed at the Casualty Clearing Station especially early wound excision of devitalised tissue which could be harbouring infection. Lastly, soldiers with 'non survivable' wounds would be given morphine to relieve pain and put aside to die. Transport down the line from the main dressing station was by horse drawn or motor ambulance. Casualty Clearing Stations were usually on a railway siding so once surgical patients had made sufficient recovery they were sent by ambulance train, or if near a river on hospital barges, to the base hospital to make room for further casualties. From there they would go to General hospitals from where they would hope to be sent home i.e. to 'Blighty'. Sections of the medical staff of a field ambulance could be deployed to look after the wounded at any stage of evacuation, wherever the need was greatest.

Information about the role of the 3rd WRFA throughout the war has been obtained from its war diary in the national archives and from the personal diaries of James Mackinnon, John Richardson, and Henry Welsby. The ambulance was initially commanded in France by Lt. Col. John W. Stokes with Major James Mackinnon second in command. John Stokes died in February, 1916 and James Mackinnon was promoted to Lt. Col. taking over command of the unit for virtually the rest of the war. It is clear that the ambulance was active in the major battles of the Somme, Ypres, Arras, Cambrai and Valenciennes and many of its members were decorated for bravery, James Mackinnon being awarded the DSO, Robert Stark and William Allen the Military Cross and Bar and 20 others the Military Medal. Capt. William Barnsley Allen, a graduate of Sheffield University Medical School, became one of the most decorated soldiers of the war being awarded the VC, DSO, and MC and Bar. In between the fighting there were however periods of leisure, James Mackinnon recounting visits to churches and *'riding along the River Lys at a fine canter'*, also *'an improvised band of the ambulance playing selections one evening'*. One afternoon he went *'a-frogging to a pond 2 1/2 miles away and caught 40. E. F. Skinner* (a physician at the Sheffield Royal Hospital) *was a picture in shirt and monocle walking amongst nettles - the following day had frogs for lunch – delightful'*. There are other accounts of a cricket match between the officers and other ranks, a stage show by the *'Tykes'* which was *'very good'*, a football match between officers and sergeants and even a divisional horse show *'their exhibits being nowhere'*. Despite these moments however, they coped with enormous numbers of casualties from the fighting, some measure of which can be seen from Mackinnon's diary *'in 6 weeks, round about Ypres, 50,000 casualties passed through about 10 field ambulances'*. There must also have been many moments of personal loss for members of the ambulance. One of these involved Ernest Finch, then an assistant surgeon at Sheffield Royal Infirmary, who received word that Jack Gwynne, son of Dr. Gwynne of Fulwood and one of the 14 Sheffield graduates in 1914, had arrived not far from his sector and rode over to see him and got there just in time for his funeral.

A particular insight can be obtained from these diaries as to the great diversity and severity of wounds confronting a field ambulance surgeon. Mackinnon records *'called at 5 a.m. by Finch* (? to give anaesthetic) *bullet wound Rt. temporal region. Haemorrhage of middle meningeal artery. Finch opened up skull, tied artery, Haemorrhage had been severe. Left theatre with fairly good pulse -60. Died at 11 a.m. At post-mortem tiny wound entrance underneath and behind left mastoid. Bullet had passed right through brain'*. Then a few days later *'called to help Finch tying femoral artery–shrapnel wound through lower thigh at upper end. Patient had lost a lot of blood. Finch first transfused. Pulse rapid and thready'*. This seemed a successful operation but later: *'case – femoral artery; tied 2 days ago going down hill'*. On another occasion *'received a shrapnel wound of left chest above heart. Finch removed bullet lying underneath skin at back'*. The noise of battle is described by John Richardson, a stretcher bearer in the 3rd WRFA, who was at Estaires when at 5 a.m. 1,700 guns along a front of 15 miles started firing. He says it was *'simply hell. No one can realise the number of shells fired. It was like a continuous role of bad thunder'* and it went on for 11 hours. On another occasion *'the bombardment is terrible. Simply one long buzz of shells. They make a very curious scream as they come and then go off with a rattle'*. John Richardson in his diary gives vent to the frustrations of a stretcher bearer *'another poor devil died here this morning. Had his leg amputated as soon as he came in but he had gone too far. They have to lie so long* (in no man's land) *before we can deal with them that accounts for so many unsuccessful operations'*. Again there were welcome distractions *'wrestling on horseback. Great Fun'*. The effects of gas are described by

Henry Welsby in his diary *'could not sleep because my head was too bad. Temp rising. Effects of gas I got two days ago. Determined to carry on with my duties until I cannot do so any longer. Gas has a very bad effect on the lungs, making one vomit slime'.* Then *'W. Smith killed. God! who's next? When will it all end? This war is making me an old man. In the midst of life we are in Death. God help and comfort his loved ones at home'.* He also describes the sheer enormity of war *'An English aviator dropped a bomb on the station hitting a train full of dynamite at Quesnes just as a train of Bosche (Germans) was going through. 2,000 German soldiers were killed outright and the pilot and observer of the plane were killed in the fearful explosion'.*

The 1/3 West Riding Field Ambulance obviously possessed a great spirit of camaraderie which is exhibited in a bivouac journal published regularly in manuscript form throughout the war called 'The Lead Swinger'. This contained articles, poems, cartoons and sketches which were all published under 'nom de plumes' or as they preferred 'nom de guerre'. The leading lights in this publication were the two Northend brothers, Ernest and William. Ernest was the editor and went under the name of 'Castorius Iodinus' and William, a talented artist, was responsible for the cartoons and drawings under the name of 'Dug-out'. Their story is told elsewhere in this book. At the end of the war 'The Lead Swinger' was published as a souvenir in 3 volumes for the members of the Field Ambulance.

Drawing by W. F. Northend of the Field Ambulance at Herzeele, Northern France

It is clear that the field ambulance saw extensive action both in Northern France and Belgium throughout the war. In September 1916, at Clairfaye on one day they admitted over 900 cases of which 650 were evacuated and 250 returned to duty, 30% had bullet wounds and there were 50 cases of shell shock, nevertheless every soldier received a hot drink and a hot meal on arrival. Later that month, on one occasion, they admitted 50 gas casualties which they treated with Atropine subcutaneously and oxygen and inhalations of ammonia to lessen the cough. Throughout the war they dealt with cases of German measles, scabies, infective jaundice, diphtheria, trench foot, enteric fever and no doubt many other diseases. Interestingly on the 3rd July, 1918, Capt. William Allen was admitted to the 1/2 Field Ambulance with influenza and it is possible that this was responsible for him developing the neurological disorder thought to be encephalitis lethargica which was responsible for his death some years later. The field ambulance was not demobilised until 25th June, 1919, when they left Boulogne for a dispersal camp in England. They continued to hold reunions every year, usually presided over by Lt. Col. James Mackinnon for many years, these usually being preceded by a short memorial service for their fallen comrades at the small memorial stone beside the official war memorial in Weston Park, Sheffield.

Derek Cullen

Casualties of the British Expeditionary Force, France and Flanders, 1914-18

During the Great War, the British Expeditionary Force in France and Flanders sustained 2.7 million battle casualties. Just over a quarter were never seen by the medical services. These men had been killed, were missing or had been taken prisoner. Of those who lived to be treated, 5.4% of the total number of casualties died from wounds sustained.

At the outbreak of the war, a system was put in place to evacuate casualties from regimental aid posts (RAP) close to the front line, to field ambulances and then to casualty clearing stations before transferring them by hospital train to base hospitals on the French coast, where they would undergo definitive surgery. It took far too long to reach these base hospitals. Filthy wounds sustained in the heavily fertilised fields of France and Flanders were contaminated by organisms responsible for gas gangrene. As a result, many patients reached base hospitals with established gangrene and lost their limbs or their lives. It was necessary to operate on such patients before they were sent by train to the base.

Casualty clearing stations were generally out of range of shell fire and yet close enough to the front to be reached relatively quickly by motor ambulance wagon convoy. Clearing stations increasingly took on the role of performing major limb and life-saving surgery before patients were sent by train to base hospitals. By 1917, 30% of the wounded underwent definitive surgery at clearing stations. During the Third Battle of Ypres in 1917, no fewer than 61,423 soldiers were operated on in casualty clearing stations.

The clinical problems presented by huge numbers of casualties during the Great War led to the emergence of surgical specialties, including orthopaedic surgery. In 1914, surgeon Robert Jones from Liverpool visited hospitals in France, and pointed out that there were far too many soldiers with musculo-skeletal wounds whose initial management had been poor, and who were blocking hospital beds in France and in Britain. These men were neither fit for return to military duty, nor for discharge to civilian life. Jones notified the Director General of Army Medical Services, Sir Alfred Keogh, about this state of affairs and this led to Jones opening an experimental orthopaedic unit in Alder Hay in Liverpool in early 1915, segregating soldiers with orthopaedic wounds for the first time. So successful was this unit, that Jones opened the first of many Orthopaedic Centres on the site of the Hammersmith Workshop in Shepherd's Bush, London, in 1916. This centre provided the surgical expertise to treat late orthopaedic problems such as mal-union or non-union of fractures, whilst at the same time providing a curative workshop by giving men an occupation which both restored function and improved morale. By 1918, there were 17 orthopaedic centres around Britain with a total of 20,000 beds.

Jones also made a major contribution to the management of the most serious acute orthopaedic wound of the Great War, the compound fracture of the femur, caused by bullet or shell fragment. He introduced the Thomas Splint to immobilise fractures of the femur. Invented by his uncle, Welsh medical practitioner Hugh Owen Thomas, and used by him to immobilise knee joints affected by tuberculosis, the Thomas Splint proved to be equally effective in stabilising fractures of the femur. Jones made the Thomas Splint available on the Western Front with the help and encouragement of his colleague Henry Gray. Before the war, Gray was surgeon to the Aberdeen Royal Infirmary and he spent three and a half years in France, first in charge of a group of base hospitals in Rouen, and then as consulting surgeon to the British 3rd Army. He was widely regarded as one of the most capable military surgeons. Gray documented a mortality of 80% for compound fractures of the femur in 1914 and 1915. Splints for immobilising these fractures in the early months of the war were ineffective and uncontrolled movement of the bone ends at the fracture site led to excessive blood loss. As a result, soldiers reached clearing stations in a shocked state and unfit to withstand the major wound excision necessary to save their limbs and lives.

During the Battle of Arras which began on Easter Monday in April 1917, Gray collected a series of 1,009 compound fractures of the femur in a six week period, all of whom had their fractures treated using a Thomas Splint. Before the Battle of Arras, using inadequate splints the mortality of this type of wound in clearing stations alone was 50%. Using the Thomas Splint at Arras, the mortality in clearing stations was 15.6%, a reduction of more than 30%. All but 5% of patients were fit to undergo wound excision. Gray wrote a book in 1918 entitled 'The Early Treatment of War Wounds' in which he summarised the management of a wide variety of wounds. This book was widely regarded as a definitive work on war surgery which epitomised the advancing knowledge of the period. Indeed, Gray laid down the principles of war surgery, which are as relevant today in Camp Bastion in Afghanistan as they were in France and Flanders 1914-18.

Tom Scotland

James Mackinnon DSO, MB, ChB.

James Mackinnon was born in Glasgow in 1876. He was educated at Allan Glenn's School and Glasgow University, graduating MB, ChB in 1900. After house appointments at the Victoria Infirmary and Leith Fever Hospital in Glasgow he started in practice in West Hartlepool but moved to Sheffield in 1903 to join a General Practice in Pitsmoor as assistant to Dr. Longbottom. He later succeeded to the Practice. In 1912, he joined a local field ambulance as an Officer in the Territorial Army. On the outbreak of war he was immediately called up as second in command of the 3rd West Riding Field Ambulance. The Ambulance moved to France in April 1915 and he was given command with the rank of Lieutenant Colonel and remained as such until March 1918 when he was appointed Assistant Director of Medical Services (ADMS) to the 66th Division.

Lt. Col. James Mackinnon

He was mentioned in Despatches twice in April and November 1916, for Gallantry and Distinguished Service in the Field. In January 1917, he was awarded the DSO. for an outstanding improvement of camp sanitation. The field ambulance remained stationary for miles behind the front line for nearly a year. It had to establish First Aid Posts for the treatment and evacuation of the sick and wounded, supply Regimental Medical Officers when necessary and establish a field hospital for the admission and treatment of cases of scabies. Several hundreds of these men needed a few days treatment and the disposal of liquid and solid excreta as well as other rubbish became an urgent problem. He solved this by designing and constructing an incinerator which disposed of all excreta and at the same time producing sufficient heat to provide a drying room for the men's clothes and enough hot water for washing and baths without producing any offensive smell.

On the 5th July 1917, he married Irene Moore, daughter of the Reverend John Moore and Mrs. Mary Moore. They had 4 children (2 sons and 2 daughters). After the war, he returned to the General Practice in Pitsmoor with another officer of the field ambulance, Major (Dr.) R. A. Stark as his partner. An Old Comrades Association was formed in connection with the local Territorial Medical Units with Dr. Mackinnon as

President. He was also elected Chairman of the local Medical Committee from 1924 and he held this office until the National Health Service was inaugurated in 1948. He had been Chairman of the Sheffield Branch of the British Medical Association and was Chairman of the No. 1 National Service Medical Board from 1939 to 1952. He was also President of the Sheffield Caledonian Society for 7 years and was a past President of the Sheffield Medico-Chirurgical Society.

In spite of his professional work he managed to lead an athletic life almost to the end. As an undergraduate he was a member of the Glasgow University Swimming team. He was also a keen tennis player. Later he was a founder member of the Sheffield Medical Golfing Society. Playing off a single figure handicap, he was a member of Lindrick and Wortley Golf Clubs. A keen curler, he was 'Skip of the Rink' of Sheffield Curling Club. He was a stern disciplinarian but also a great family man who loved nothing more than a game of beach cricket on family holidays. He held strongly to the Presbyterian Faith and was a Deacon of St. James Presbyterian Church in Pitsmoor. Finally he was described as one of the first men of his profession who put duty above everything else and never spared himself.

John Mackinnon

Cartoon of Lt. Col. James Mackinnon
by Pipsqueak from the Lead Swinger

The changing management of abdominal wounds during the Great War; from 'laissez faire' to urgent surgical intervention and lessons relearned!

At the start of the Great War, patients with penetrating wounds of the abdomen were generally dealt with by 'expectant management' and the vast majority died. Those who did survive were probably mistakenly believed to have penetrating wounds, while in fact only the abdominal wall was involved and the peritoneum was intact. The first successful bowel resection was not performed until 18th March 1915, when surgeon Owen Richards removed 6 feet of small bowel from a soldier with multiple perforations caused by a shell fragment.

Throughout the nineteenth century, management of abdominal wounds had been mostly conservative. Certainly in the first half of the century, when there was no general anaesthesia, surgeons had neither the skill nor the means to perform abdominal surgery. The advent of general anaesthesia in time for the Crimean War made little difference to this state of affairs. Even by the Second Boer War, 1899-1902, surgery for penetrating abdominal wounds was rarely performed. Sir William MacCormac, Consulting Surgeon to the British Army, expressed the view *'In this war a man wounded in the abdomen dies if he is operated upon and remains alive if left in peace'*. This view was probably based on poor results from the American Civil War and Franco-Prussian War.

The first real progress with penetrating abdominal wounds came in 1904-5 during the Russo-Japanese War, when Russian surgeon Vera Gedroits, working in a Red Cross Hospital Train close to the front, operated on 168 patients very soon after they had been wounded. Her results were good, but were either ignored or went unnoticed in the west. The lessons she had learned had to be 'rediscovered' during the Great War. Early intervention was of paramount importance. Owen Richards operated on 9 patients with a perforated bowel in the first few months of the Great War. All but 2 died. The two patients who survived had undergone very early laparotomy and bowel resection. Surgeon Cuthbert Wallace realised the importance of early intervention, and he made the important discovery that bleeding was the main cause of early death, within hours of being wounded. Infection (peritonitis) was responsible for late deaths. Further work revealed that these wounds were of such a nature that spontaneous cessation of bleeding would not have taken place. It was also clear that multiple injuries to both bowel and to blood vessels could occur. Wounds of the buttocks and back were frequently associated with abdominal wounds, so patients with such wounds were sent to clearing stations where expertise in the management of abdominal wounds was available. Captains John Fraser and Hamilton Drummond reported a series of 300 cases of penetrating abdominal wound, and also found time to do experimental work on what surgical technique should be employed to perform an anastomosis; on why the intestine dilated after surgery (paralytic ileus); and on the details of blood supply to the intestine. They also examined how the position of a wound in the small intestine affected outcome.

Audit is a part of the evaluation of every surgeon's activity today, but there was little time for audit during the Great War – not so for patients with penetrating abdominal wounds. The time taken to get the casualty to an operating facility was crucial and was monitored. The average time was 6 hours; after 12 hours delay, the mortality was higher; after 24 hours, it was very high indeed. Wounds of the small intestine that only required suturing carried the best prognosis; the position of the wound in the abdomen was important. Wounds of the upper abdomen had a better prognosis, while wounds of lower abdomen had a poorer prognosis because more bowel was involved. Wounds associated with chest damage formed a very serious category indeed. If the pulse rate was <100, the prognosis was better; if the pulse was <120, the chances of survival were reduced; if the pulse was >120, there was very little chance of survival.

Casualties with abdominal wounds were evacuated preferentially from Regimental Aid Posts (RAP) to Advanced Dressing Station (ADS) and placed in a motor ambulance wagon, which could be heated. Warming the casualty helped to improve the general condition of the casualty in transit to a designated casualty clearing station, to be operated upon by an experienced surgeon. Upon arrival, patients were assessed for their suitability for surgery. For example, if the clinical condition was so bad that death would almost certainly occur then there was no point undertaking surgery. If the wound was in the upper right quadrant of the abdomen and the patient's condition was stable, with no evidence of on-going bleeding, then the most likely diagnosis was a liver wound which carried a relatively good prognosis without intervention. Progress in the understanding of resuscitation and safer anaesthesia also contributed to increasing success.

One of the most serious wounds was a penetrating wound of both chest and abdomen. This occurred in 12% of abdominal wounds and 9% of chest wounds. Clinical experience led to the establishment of clear guidelines for surgery, and the results improved significantly. During 1916 the recovery rate from these wounds was only 18%; by 1917 it was 49% and by 1918 was 67%. Even today with intensive therapy units and all available supportive measures, thoraco-abdominal wounds carry a significant mortality.

Tom Scotland

Infectious diseases and the First World War

The impact of infectious diseases on a military conflict is well described and easy to understand. Historically, the ratio of deaths associated with infectious diseases to deaths associated with the consequences of battle has been high; for example the ratio was 10:1 during the Spanish-American war of 1898. However, the understanding of the mode of transmission of infection and the impact of disease resulted in action to limit its spread which had a profound effect on these figures. By the time of the First World War, though infection still occurred, the ratio had been dramatically reduced to 1:1. In modern warfare public health measures supported by immunisation and antimicrobial therapy together with a changing 'military style' has made death from infection very uncommon.

Why was infection such a problem?

In order to answer this question, it is important to understand how infections are transmitted and what additional opportunities for transmission occur in times of military conflict.

People living in confined quarters with close proximity to each other have a greater risk of transmitting infections spread by aerosol such as respiratory infections, including TB, meningococcal infection and influenza.

Lack of clean drinking water and safe removal of sewage and inadequate preparation of food increases risk of transmission of 'food and waterborne' infections such as dysentery, enteric fever and salmonella. Hepatitis A is spread in a similar manner.

Failure of basic hygiene in soldiers living in close quarters will provide opportunity for infestations such as body lice which can carry organisms such as those giving rise to typhus.

Rats thrived in the wet trenches and are the source of diseases such as leptospirosis.

A change in social environment and behaviour in times of war results in an increase in sexually transmitted diseases.

In 1914 there were no antimicrobials such as sulphonamides and penicillin. Vaccination was available against smallpox but there was no immunisation for the common diseases of war. However, Sir Almroth Wright did develop a vaccine against typhoid though getting this established as an obligatory vaccine for British troops was less than easy. This is surprising as the Australian and United States armies made inoculation compulsory and Germany inoculated all prisoners of war against typhoid. Citing the example of the Second Boer War, during which many soldiers died from easily preventable diseases, Wright was convinced of the benefits to the Army but there was reluctance amongst the higher authorities in Britain for it to be compulsory. Nonetheless, under the guidance of the medical officers, the vast majority of the armed forces did in fact receive typhoid vaccination and the incidence of disease was dramatically lower than in previous conflicts; it was only 2% of the incidence in the Boer War a few years before.

Tetanus was a serious infection arising from contaminated wounds but the first immunisation (toxoid) for this infection was not produced until 1924, after the First World War.

Who was responsible for public health intervention to minimise risk of infectious diseases in the war?

Organisation of public health intervention was under the auspices of the Royal Army Medical Corps (RAMC). A great deal of the organisational structure of the RAMC was designed to address the more obvious consequences of war for those injured as a result of the conflict including evacuation of injured personnel and provision of optimum management, medical and surgical, within a first aid or hospital setting. However, many lessons had been learned from previous conflicts regarding infection, most recently the Boer War. 'Undoubtedly the most important function performed by a Medical Officer was disease prevention'. (Doctors in the Great War, Ian R. Whitehead). Maintenance of the health of the fighting force was fundamental. In an era when reducing risk of infection (public health) and reducing the risk of transmission if infection did occur (isolation and quarantine) were the backbone of limiting infectious diseases, much could be done to achieve this. The public health aspects also included maintenance of good hygiene which was also recognised as being absolutely crucial. The involvement of the Regimental Medical Officer with the front line troops enabled him to judge the fitness of the men at daily sick parades. It was a challenging task requiring clinical judgement backed up by wisdom and emotional toughness. It was necessary to maintain the fighting force and allow 'off sick' only those who were clearly unable to fight.

The role of the Regimental Medical Officer included:

Getting latrines erected

Checking latrines daily

Checking food supplies

Ensuring basic rules of hygiene were being followed in kitchens

Taking measures to prevent fly infestation

Inspecting men for scabies and lice

Endeavouring to keep the men's clothing and bodies clean by making bathing facilities available where possible

Identifying any contagious diseases, isolation of cases and establishing means of control

How did the RAMC institute public health measures?

Sanitary discipline

At the top of the structure was the 'Sanitary Committee' with a senior combatant officer as President, reflecting the high priority at all levels given to control of infection. Between this committee and the front line was a 'Sanitary Section'. At the front line there was the same underlying guiding principle for sanitary measures inasmuch that it was the Officer in Command who was actually the person responsible i.e. infection control was given the highest priority within the Army to ensure that it did not get neglected. The Officer in Command would be advised by the relevant representative of the Director of Medical Services. Each unit had a team of between 3 and 9 men (depending on its size) for sanitary duties, and additionally 2-4 trained RAMC men under the supervision of a corporal who were on water duties. Divisional sanitary sections were established in October 1914 and responsibilities included:

checking sanitation of towns (often very poor)

burning rubbish

disposal of faecal material

filling in latrines

ensuring the men only drank from safe water sources

disinfecting clothes

cleaning up after the military had left

However, disease was never far away and the constant movement of men in the Somme in 1916 resulted in a breakdown in sanitary measures and an outbreak of dysentery.

Rat control

Not surprisingly, rats thrived in trenches. Rats are the source of diseases such as leptospirosis, a bacterial infection which can cause severe illness with jaundice and kidney failure. The bacteria are present in the rats' urine which would soil the sodden trenches. The bacteria are acquired by the troops by the leptospira passing through damaged skin or mucus membranes. Education about control of rats, for example with traps, was part of training of all involved in sanitation.

The sanitary work of RMOs, so often underestimated by wartime critics of the RAMC, was of great value.

Personal Hygiene

Lice were common where personal hygiene was poor, washing of clothes was neglected or not possible and men lived in close proximity to each other. They were almost universal in the front lines – infestation of the officers and men ran at about 97%. Lice were the scourge of armies in the field and were, after the end of the First World War, recognised as being the source of organisms giving rise to relapsing fever and typhus. The first description of trench fever was made by Major J. Graham in September 1915. The illness of trench fever would last about 5 days and may relapse several times but it often left the sufferer debilitated for many weeks. 'During 1917 ... an army of 1,000,000 would lose in a year at least 45,000 casualties from trench fever. Of these casualties, at least 80% would lose on an average, at least three months off duty.' (Of lice and men – http://www.the-field-ambulance.org/of-lice--men.html) The link between lice and trench foot was finally established in 1918. Though trench foot can be prevented by keeping the feet clean, warm and dry, this was not easy to achieve in wet, cold trenches. The key preventive measure, which was established in the First World War, was for regular foot inspections. The simple system of pairing up soldiers and making each responsible for the feet of the other went a long way to establishing control.

Further evidence for the common presence of bartonella and rickettsia in troops has recently been shown. A study of lice found in a mass grave of Napoleon's soldiers in Vilnius, Lithuania using modern PCR technology found that 3 of the 5 lice were infected with Bartonella quintana (the agent of trench fever) and 7 of 35 soldiers had evidence of the same organism present in their dental pulp (i.e. they were infected); a further 3 had Rickettsia prowazekii (the agent causing epidemic typhus) identified in the same site. (Raoult et al. Evidence for louse-transmitted diseases in soldiers of Napoleon's grand army in Vilnius. J. Infect Dis 2006: 193; 192-120). Additionally personal hygiene was important in limiting other problems such as fungal skin infections and scabies.

Laboratory support against infectious diseases

Diagnosis of specific infectious agents is a key factor in enabling optimal management of an infectious disease. Bacteriologists played a bigger part in the First World War than in any previous military encounter with the first mobile bacteriology laboratory arriving on the Western Front in 1914.

Other specific infections related to the First World War

Venereal Infections

These did not receive the attention that they should have had. The annual wastage of manpower due to venereal infection was as high as 287 per 1,000 amongst some imperial troops which reflected a truly massive drain of manpower. Lord Kitchener had emphasised the importance of self restraint and a law was passed (Defence of the Realm Act) to make it an offence to solicit, invite or perform sexual intercourse with any member of the Armed Forces. However this probably had little effect on the incidence. Additionally another 'stick' approach to try to limit infections was punishment. If a soldier had a venereal infection and concealed the matter, he could be court-martialled, imprisoned and have 2 years hard labour. If he reported the infection to his medical officer, he would go to hospital but lost all pay and emoluments and his wife lost her separation allowance during the time that he was confined. The punitive approach had little impact on the incidence of disease. Eventually before the end of the war, despite a strong moral lobby resisting its introduction, prophylactic self administered disinfectants became available in Britain, which did have an impact on the number of cases of venereal infection.

Influenza

The world wide pandemic of influenza (Spanish flu) started in the spring of 1918 with further waves of infection in the autumn and winter of that year. Despite much scientific endeavour it was not until 1933 that the influenza virus was identified. There was an influenza vaccine which was used on the British troops but it probably provided little or no benefit in disease prevention. The most common complication of influenza is pneumonia which can be due to the virus or to secondary bacterial infection. The influenza and the associated pneumonia proved to put an enormous strain on the medical services in 1918 with 226,615 cases being reported by the Army in the spring outbreak and a further 93,670 incapacitated and there were 5,555 deaths in the November and December outbreak. Therapy was limited – 'physicians tried everything they knew, everything they had ever heard of, from the ancient art of bleeding patients, to administering oxygen, to developing new vaccines and sera (chiefly against what we now call Hemophilus influenzae – a name derived from the fact that it was originally considered the etiological agent – and several types of pneumococci). Only one therapeutic measure, transfusing blood from recovered patients to new victims, showed any hint of success.

Demographic studies of death in soldiers from Australia has recently demonstrated a strong inverse correlation between length of service and mortality risk from pneumonia-influenza during 1918-19. It was 9 times higher amongst soldiers enlisting in 1918 compared with the 1914/15 cohort. The protective effect from longer service probably reflected increased acquired immunity to influenza viruses and to the endemic bacterial strains that caused secondary pneumonia which was responsible for most of the deaths during the pandemic (Shanks et al. Mortality risk factors during the 1918-19 influenza pandemic in the Australian army. J Infect Dis. 2010; 201: 1880-9). It seems likely that there would have been a similar protective effect from longer service also in British soldiers.

It is accepted that there were more deaths worldwide from the influenza epidemic at the end and after the war than deaths resulting from the war itself – the estimated number of deaths from the influenza epidemic is 40 million.

Sheffield infectious diseases admissions before the First World War (1900-14)

The Sheffield City Hospitals annual reports from 1900 to 1914 show the main categories of infection were scarlet fever, enteric fever and diphtheria. There is therefore a picture of the background admissions with infections prior to the First World War. The figures for these infections in 1914 were:

Scarlet fever	2,343 cases	mortality rate 2.9% (87.5% < 15 yrs age)
Enteric fever	83 cases	mortality rate 12%
Diphtheria	606 cases	mortality rate 5.1%

There were additionally other infectious diseases in Sheffield prior to the war:

Smallpox – intermittent cases (60 in 1904 with a mortality rate of 5.8%) but none in 1914.

Measles – not every year but 190 in 1911 with a mortality rate of 14.2%; only 5 cases in 1914, 2 of whom died.

Poliomyelitis – only reported in 1912 when there were 18 cases with no deaths.

Typhus – one case in 1908 and another in 1912 who died.

TB – not reported in annual reports until 1908 after which there was an annual increase reaching 662 in 1914 with a mortality rate of 14.7%.

By 1914 the majority of infectious diseases were managed at Lodge Moor Hospital. The daily average number of cases of infectious diseases in each hospital for that year was:

Lodge Moor Hospital (424 beds in 1914)	335.4
Crimicar Lane Hospital (mainly for TB)	27.0
Winter Street Hospital („)	76.0
Moor End Hospital	25.8

The lack of specific active management for these infections resulted in prolonged periods of isolation. The average duration of admissions for the years 1904-13 were:

Scarlet Fever   46.7 days

Enteric Fever   45.6 days

Diptheria   40.4 days

Sheffield infectious diseases admissions during the First World War amongst military personnel.

Comprehensive data on admissions during the First World War is not available in the archives. Admission and discharge data from Lodge Moor Hospital (24th August 1914 to 28th December 1919) and Winter Street Hospital (most of the records available January 1916 to February 1919) are available and have recently been reviewed (Dr Michael Collins – personal communication). The data for Lodge Moor Hospital and Winter Street are from the admission and discharge books specifically for military personnel.

It is probable, from the information which is still available, that Lodge Moor Hospital remained the major infectious diseases hospital during the war years though some cases were admitted to the other hospitals and many non infectious war related diagnoses were recorded at Winter Street. It is quite possible that many of these 'trauma related' war diagnoses may have had some 'infectious' complications but this is not recorded. It is difficult to know how many of the infectious diseases amongst military men were truly related to their involvement in the war rather than having been acquired in Sheffield after their return but probably a small number.

Of the 335 admissions to Lodge Moor Hospital between 1914 and 1919 there were 10 deaths (4 cerebrospinal fever, 1 each of pyuria, pneumococcal meningitis, pneumonia, malaria, diphtheria and purulent bronchitis). There were also 187 admissions during the same period of 'contacts' who will probably have been admitted for reasons of observation or control of spread of infection. The specific diagnoses to Lodge Moor Hospital for which there were greater than 20 admissions included:

Enteric fever	59
Scarlet fever	81
Diphtheria	48
Measles	25
German measles	46
Cerebrospinal fever/ meningitis	30

Most infectious diseases have a short incubation period and thus may have been acquired in Sheffield after return. This would include scarlet fever (1-3 days), diphtheria (2-5 days), measles (10 days) and influenza (1-3 days). Typhoid and paratyphoid (3-30 days, usually 10-14) could have been acquired locally or brought back from the Front while malaria (7-30 days but can be many months) must have been brought back from abroad as it does not occur as a locally transmitted infection. However, it is quite possible that some of the more common infections were actually acquired in the military environment and the clinical illness became manifest a few days or weeks after return to Sheffield. A good example of this is cerebrospinal fever caused by *Neisseria meningitidis* infection. The number of admissions due to cerebrospinal fever was higher amongst the military personnel than the background rate before the war. It is recognised that a higher rate of colonisation with meningococcus occurs in those living close to each other for example in barracks (only a small proportion of those 'colonised' with the organism will actually get 'clinical disease'). A similar case could be made with regard to *Haemolytic streptococcus* colonisation and development of scarlet fever and also to *Corynebacterium diphtheriae* colonisation and the development of diphtheria.

Measles is a surprising diagnosis to be recorded in persons of military age as it is such a highly infectious disease that it is nearly always seen in children and extremely rarely in adults; it is possible that some of these cases may have been due to another virus which presented in a measles like manner – the diagnoses were clinical rather than laboratory based.

In Winter Street Hospital there were very few recorded admissions of scarlet fever, diphtheria or enteric fever and only occasional cases of measles. Infectious diseases which were recorded and were probably related to the war included 17 cases of trench fever between December 1917 and May 1918 and 15 cases of malaria over the same time period (2 admissions for trench foot and 2 cases of malaria recorded between January 1916 and December 1917 would also have probably been related to the war). Presumably the main repatriation of troops occurred during the last phases of the war and hence the timing of these medical problems.

The rise in influenza admissions in 1918 from 3 to 15 is consistent with the pandemic occurring during that year. (Much of the source data about RAMC and control of infection during the First World War is from Doctors in the Great War by Ian R. Whitehead; Pen and Sword Military, 1999)

Michael McKendrick

Percy Wood and Arthur Simpson
lifelong friends

Percy Wood was born into a very poor Sheffield family in 1896. At the outbreak of the Great War in 1914 he joined the services at the age of 18 years where he met Arthur Simpson. They were to become lifelong friends. Arthur was five years older then Percy, his entry to the services having been delayed until he had completed his indenture as an apprentice 'Weaver Overlooker' at a woollen mill in Bradford. When younger he had wanted to train as a doctor but his family could not afford the fees. He and Percy joined the R.A.M.C. training at Strensall near York and became company buglers. After their training they were posted to Gell Street Barracks in Sheffield and were probably billeted with the civilian population.

Percy Wood and Arthur Simpson

After further training at Clipstone, Notts, they were posted to France with the 3rd West Riding Field Ambulance and served together on the front line and in field hospitals. Arthur actually recovered his own brother, Bernard, whose legs had been injured, from the battlefield. A decision had been made by the surgeon to amputate both Bernard's legs and Arthur tried unsuccessfully to prevent this. However, despite his bilateral amputation, Bernard recovered and thereafter led a comparatively independent lifestyle. Arthur, himself, was gassed during the war and lost his sight for about three weeks, fortunately making a good recovery and returning to duty. Both friends however, survived the war and were discharged from the army within a few months of each other. Arthur was discharged in November 1918 having just been recommended for officer training. Percy was discharged early in 1919.

Following discharge from the army, Percy married Florence May Styring and they had two sons. Like many other servicemen he had great difficulty finding a job, being eventually employed in 1923 as a labourer at 'Steel, Peach and Tozer' in Rotherham on the present site of 'Magna'. As they did not have a company doctor or nurse he also acted as a First Aid Man. After many years of trying, he finally managed to get employment as an ambulance attendant on Sheffield Corporation Ambulance Service (SCAS). In 1939, he decided to emigrate with his family to South Africa and was due to embark on September 7th but this was cancelled on the 4th September due to the outbreak of the Second World War.

Arthur married Emily Munton and he returned to work in the woollen mills in Bradford after the war. In December 1940, he became very concerned about his friend Percy's safety following the Sheffield Blitz and decided to cycle from Bradford to Sheffield to see if he needed help. However, he could only get to the outskirts of the city because there was so much broken glass and he had to preserve his tyres as there was no other means of transport. He therefore unwillingly returned home not knowing that his friend, Percy, had been killed by enemy action whilst on duty with the Sheffield City Ambulance Service.

Eric Wood

William Barnsley Allen
VC, DSO, MC and Bar
Sheffield's 'Forgotten Hero'

William Barnsley Allen was born at 14 Botanical Road, Sheffield, on 8th June 1892. The family later lived at Southgrove Road and Endcliffe Vale Road. He was educated at Worksop College, and Sheffield University Medical School and qualified MB, ChB with Honours in 1914 and was awarded the Kaye Scholarship, the University Gold Medal in Pathology, as well as three other prizes for academic distinction. He was appointed to the Royal Hospital as a house physician, but on 8th August 1914, four days after the declaration of war, he enlisted in the RAMC, being gazetted a lieutenant. In August 1916, he was awarded the Military Cross, and a month later the Victoria Cross for his heroic action at Mesnil on the Somme, the citation for which was:-

'Date of Bravery 3 September 1916. For most conspicuous bravery and devotion to duty. When gun detachments were unloading high explosive ammunition from wagons which had just come up, the enemy suddenly began to shell the battery position. The first shell fell on one of the limbers, exploded the ammunition and caused several casualties. Capt. Allen saw the occurrence and at once, with utter disregard of danger, ran straight across the open, under heavy shell fire, commenced

From left to right, William Barnsley Allen, John W. Stokes, James Mackinnon, and Robert Stark

dressing the wounded, and undoubtedly by his promptness saved many of them from bleeding to death. He was himself hit four times during the first hour by pieces of shells, one of which fractured two of his ribs, but he never even mentioned this at the time, and coolly went on with his work till the last man was dressed and safely removed. He then went over to another battery and tended a wounded officer. It was only when this was done that he returned to his dug-out and reported his own injury'.

Twice in September and in October that year he was Mentioned in Despatches. In 1917 he was awarded a Bar to the MC and in 1918 he was decorated with the Distinguished Service Order. At the end of the war he was promoted to Captain, and received a permanent commission. For a few years he served in India, where he contracted malaria and dysentery. Following his return to England, he suffered from pleurisy and from encephalitis lethargica – 'sleepy sickness' – a mysterious but devastating illness of epidemic proportions which is thought to have killed up to half a million people world-wide in the 1920s. William Allen resigned his commission in 1923, with the rank of Major. He died on 27th August, 1933, aged 41 years and is buried at Earnley Parish Church, Sussex. He is little known or remembered in his native Sheffield although Somme Barracks on West Street has a room devoted to his memory, in which are displayed a framed photograph, his citation and replicas of his Victoria Cross and other medals.

David Baldwin

Lydia Henry
(1891-1985)

The turmoil of 1914-19, catapulted many young people into unprecedented situations and thrust women into areas of work and responsibilities previously closed to them. Among such young women was Lydia Henry.

In 1914, Lydia (or Leila as she was called) was one of very few women medical students in Sheffield. She was well on in her course. Many staff and male students enlisted and the remaining medical students worked even harder than before, taking over some of the duties normally carried out by interns. The disruption to hospitals, the extra work, and difficulties of accommodation complicated her later student years but, in 1916, she was one of the first two women to graduate in Medicine from Sheffield University. The day after graduation, she started as a house surgeon in Sheffield Royal Infirmary. A munitions factory nearby created an upsurge of extra work. Output was under pressure and more women were working in munitions. Safety measures were rudimentary with a resulting stream of accidents. Dr Henry tells of a 15 year old girl, admitted with a fatal degree of poisoning due to painting aircraft wings and licking the brushes. The danger had not been understood. She also describes a Zeppelin raid. It was a moonlight night and when the siren sounded she and a colleague climbed up to the roof to watch as bombs fell nearby, aiming for the factories, but hitting a row of houses. They went down to the casualty area, and soon the ambulances brought in the injured. During that year, she provided medical care for women in the country's first, free, government-sponsored, clinic for venereal diseases which was set up in Sheffield Royal Infirmary. There was a great need because of the civilian disruption in the heavily industrialised areas.

Leila had been born in 1891, brought up initially in Dufftown in Banffshire but family circumstances brought her to Sheffield in 1906, where her widowed mother had been appointed Vice-Principal to the City (Teacher) Training College. She attended Sheffield High School for Girls, before matriculating in Medicine in Sheffield University. After her intern year, Dr Henry served more directly in the war by joining the Scottish Women's Hospitals Service in France in June 1917 until the Spring of 1919. This was a remarkable organisation which deserves better recognition. It doesn't appear in British Army records as it was never officially part of the British Army.

Scottish Women's Hospital Committee

The organisation was set up by Dr Elsie Inglis in Edinburgh, one of the very early women pioneer doctors, who had qualified with great difficulty in 1891 before any Universities would matriculate women. In August 1914, women could not enlist as medical officers in the Forces and Dr Inglis had the idea of forming a (civilian) hospital unit staffed entirely by women – orderlies, porters, cooks and administrators as well as nurses and doctors. The War Office ridiculed the idea but Dr Inglis persisted. Several European countries, aware of their grossly inadequate medical services for war injured, showed interest and units were initially set up in Serbia and in France. A 13th Century Abbey, at Royaumont, about 30 Km north of Paris was offered to the women to be run under the auspices of the French Red Cross. Matters moved quickly. Publicity was energetic, money was raised (a lot of it by suffragettes), equipment was gathered, and, by December 1914, the advance party arrived in France to set the ancient building into some sort of order. Initially there was no heat, light or water supply but there was space and beautiful surroundings.

Lydia Henry in uniform with Croix de Guerre

By the time that Dr Henry reached Royaumont, the hospital was in full swing. Every corner and outbuilding had been pressed into service and the extensive gardens were providing produce, cultivated partly by the staff and partly by recovering patients. The work was intense if episodic. The refectory, cloisters and available space on the ground floor were used for beds as well as rooms on the next two floors. Operating theatres, X-ray equipment and stores were installed on the first floor as well as rooms for nursing the wounded. Supplies and patients had to be carried by the women up long flights of stone stairs.

Money was always a problem and much effort was put into raising funds – from UK, Canada, Australia, New Zealand and USA. Some of the women including ambulance drivers, orderlies and kitchen staff were unpaid volunteers. Most supplies including linen, instruments and surgical dressings were sent out by the organisation. The enterprise was largely controlled by the Organising Committee in Edinburgh. This group was chaired for some of the time by Mrs Russell, a very early medical woman herself, wife of the Professor of Medicine. She had been unable to enlist herself, as her youngest child was just two years old. This small boy, Scott Russell, later became the Professor of Obstetrics and Gynaecology in Sheffield, (1950-71).

The Work at Royaumont

The wounded soldiers admitted to Royaumont were mainly French, but included Arabs, Sengalese and later, some US wounded. They also admitted and treated several German prisoners. There were regular inspections by the French Red Cross and by medical personnel and the quality and high standard of the hospital was soon recognised. Its reputation was such that Professor Weinberg of the Pasteur Institute selected the unit to be one of very few to test his anti-gas gangrene serum. Good observations and records were kept and this became the subject of Dr Henry's MD (Sheffield) thesis in 1920, 'On the Treatment of War Wounds by Surgery and Anti-gas Cangrene Serum'.

The German Offensive

A subsidiary advanced hospital was established by the unit at Villers-Cotterets, some 40 miles to the east of Royaumont and very close to the firing line. It was a very primitive structure of nine huts, (previously an army camp), muddy and cold with basic facilities only. The front line was advancing nearer and in Oct 1917, March 1918 and May 1918, there were especial 'pushes' by the German Army. By May 1918 the services at the two hospitals had come under the administrative control of the Third French Army. At the end of May there was a large German advance in the region of the Aisne River, between Rheims and Soissons, very close to Villers-Cotterets. The railway line to Paris was cut as they crossed the Aisne, captured Soissons in this 'Second Battle of the Marne' and reached the Forest of Villers-Cotterets. During these crucial 4 days there was constant bombardment in the area and the hospital unit at Villers-Cotterets was isolated with a stream of casualties brought in. There was no electricity, including light, and eventually the hospital was told to evacuate. Every available wheeled vehicle was commandeered for the wounded soldiers with a few attendants. There was constant bombing as the forest roads were visible. Some staff, including Dr Henry set off walking west into the surrounding forests and villages, joining refugees as they went. They came upon an empty animal train further down the railway line and eventually got to Senlis. Gradually, vehicles, personnel and wounded, struggled into Royaumont. Over the next 15 days, there were 1,000 wounded men treated. Three theatres were working by day and two at night, on a shift system and the aftermath of this intensity continued for many weeks. Strenuous efforts were made to maintain morale. The hospital huts at Villers-Cotterets and most of the village, were completely destroyed. Both sides of the war brought reinforcements to the area, including fresh US troops and German Army Divisions formerly on the Russian front. There were offensives and counter-offensives around the area until August 1918 when the German forces were overcome. It was in the forest area very near Villers-Cotterets, in a railway carriage in Compiegne where the Armistice was signed.

Closure

The work of winding down and closing the hospital progressed over Christmas 1918 and January, and it closed in February 1919. Dr Henry and one other stayed behind to translate the case notes into French for retention in the French Army Medical Records. Altogether, between 13th January, 1915, and 26th February, 1919, the Scottish Women's Hospitals at Royaumont and Villers-Cotterets treated 10,861 patients, including 572 civilians. 7,204 operations and 188 amputations were carried out, with 184 deaths (1.7%). On 12th December, 1918, Dr. Henry together with several other members of the team at Royaument were awarded the Croix de Guerre. She was the youngest of the doctors who served at Royaumont. After 1919, Dr Henry worked in a range of medical jobs, including public health in Blackburn. In 1925 she married a distant Henry relative she had met during the war when he was serving in the Canadian Army and they settled in Canada.

In 1978, on the occasion of the 150th anniversary of the founding of the Medical School in Sheffield, Dr Henry was honoured with an Honorary DSc by the University of Sheffield. Around that time, she set out some notes and recorded some tapes of her career and especially her wartime experiences. These are in Sheffield University Archives.

Sheila Duncan

The Development of Radiology in Sheffield and WW1

Professor Wilhelm Rontgen, the German Physicist discovered X-Rays in his laboratory in Wurzburg in November 1895. After a period of further experimentation and confirmation, he announced the news of his discovery in late December 1895 which quickly spread worldwide and physicists and clinicians began to use X-Rays for experimental and diagnostic work, the latter confined to extremities because of the low output of the X-Ray tubes. The first recorded use of X-Rays in Sheffield was by Professor William Hicks, Physicist at Firth College. A report of this early work in Sheffield appeared in the British Medical Journal on February 22nd, 1896. It included images of a hand of a patient with osteoarthritis and an image of the blood vessels of a cadaveric kidney produced by Hicks in collaboration with Christopher Addison, later Professor of Anatomy. The report also described the detection of a needle in the soft tissues by X-Ray and its successful removal.

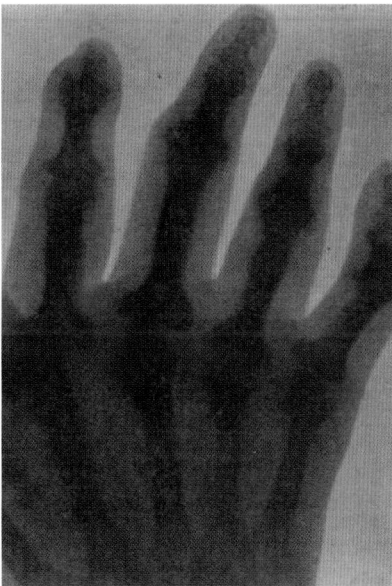

X ray of hand, Sheffield.

Gradually, X-Rays gained acceptance as a diagnostic tool in clinical practice. This factor and improvement in the apparatus led to the establishment of X-Ray departments in the main hospitals. Records confirm that the first X-Ray departments in Sheffield opened in 1906 at the Royal Hospital and the Royal Infirmary. The pioneer radiologists appointed to run these departments were Dr. William Harwood Nutt (Royal Hospital) and Dr. Rupert Hallam (Royal Infirmary). Both held the rank of Captain in the Territorial Army from 1908. It must be emphasised that the pioneer radiologists had no training in the use of X-Rays and there was no knowledge of normal radiological anatomy or of the X-Ray findings in disease. The early departments were often referred to as Electrical Departments because the work included not just X-Rays but a range of diagnostic and therapeutic procedures all requiring an electrical supply. Fluoroscopy (a real time moving image produced by X-Rays and observed on a screen) came later and the more powerful X-Ray equipment allowed the radiologists to investigate other parts of the body apart from the extremities. The radiologists were assisted by nurses and junior house staff and the first radiographer was appointed at the Royal Hospital in 1910.

X-rays and Warfare

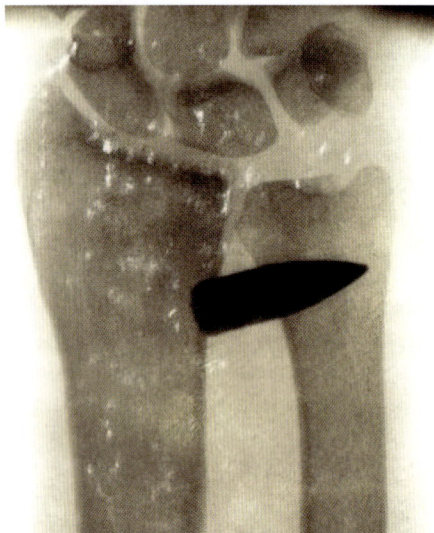

WW1 X-ray of the wrist showing a bullet

Following Rontgen's discovery in 1895, the benefits of using X-rays to detect fractures, bullets and shrapnel were quickly recognised by military surgeons. The first record of the use of X-rays in warfare was in Naples during the Italo-Abyssinian War in 1896. The British Army acquired its first X-Ray apparatus in 1896. During the second Boer War (1899–1902), portable and fixed X-Ray apparatus was employed in field hospitals. Major problems were encountered in the provision of an electrical supply to power the apparatus leading to the use of dynamos and motor engines. Reports of advances in the successful use of X-Rays in the Boer War were relayed back to Britain, in turn helping to advance the development of the new speciality of radiology. By 1910, the use of X-Rays was fully established in military as well civilian hospitals in Britain. Writing on the topic of 'Wounds and War' in 1910, William Stephenson, Professor of Military Surgery, stated that *all stationary and general hospitals and hospital ships employed in a campaign should be supplied with X-Ray apparatus'*.

Madame Curie in her X-Ray car

An important role was played in France during WW1 by Marie Curie in the development of mobile X-Ray units close to the battlefield. Madame Curie, already famed for her discovery of polonium and radium, saw the need for X-ray equipment that could be rapidly moved and convinced motor manufacturers to adapt vehicles to create an 'X-Ray car' (also dubbed the 'petite Curie'). The car engine was used to power the X-Ray apparatus. She also established a number of training centres.

Localisation of foreign bodies using X-rays

Prior to the advent of X-rays, the only method for the detection and removal of foreign bodies was that of blind probing of wounds. Not only was this uncomfortable, it was inaccurate and increased the risk of sepsis. Of course, probing of wounds was unnecessary if there was a non-invasive method of discounting foreign bodies. X-Rays were used by military surgeons to detect bullets, shell fragments and shrapnel very soon after Rontgen's discovery. The detection or elimination of these foreign bodies allowed the surgeons to adopt a more conservative approach when dealing with wounds, the foreign body removal being delayed and carried out away from the battlefield in more ideal conditions. Although straight X-Rays proved to be accurate in the detection of foreign bodies, they did not help the surgeon in their precise localisation prior to attempted removal. This obstacle was overcome when James Mackenzie Davidson, a London based pioneer radiologist, described the cross thread method for precise localisation of metallic foreign bodies using X-Rays in 1898. This technique was used during the Boer War and WW1.

WW1 and Sheffield

The overwhelming number of wounded and ill soldiers returning from the war for treatment in Sheffield led to a major re-organisation of hospital services. The 3rd Northern General Hospital was the generic name given to all of the hospitals and convalescent centres used to treat the soldiers in Sheffield and surrounding districts. The largest hospital with approximately 1,700 beds was known as the Wharncliffe War Hospital, located at the site of what was later known as the Middlewood Hospital. This hospital opened to wounded and ill soldiers on 21st May 1915 and 37,000 soldiers were treated there during the war. Records confirm that an X-Ray department was provided and that Dr. Harwood Nutt (Royal Hospital) was the attending radiologist. The civilian hospitals such as the Royal Hospital and Royal Infirmary also provided beds for the soldiers and access to X-ray facilities. Many hospital staff had enlisted because of the war effort leaving a shortage of personnel to support the service. It should not be forgotten that many of the civilian population in Sheffield were engaged in munitions factories during WW1 and injuries sustained added to the clinical workload of the hospitals. The additional military work was not funded and put severe pressure on scarce resources. It is possible to gauge the severity of the problems by noting the following statement in the Annual Report from the Royal Hospital in 1917:
'Sixty beds were placed at the disposal of the War Office free of any cost to the Government, and no less than 1,474 wounded soldiers were treated to date. The cost of treating those

patients was the large sum of £8,923. This means a free gift to the country of that amount by the subscribers to the Hospital'.

Dr Rupert Hallam and the 3rd Northern General Hospital

Prior to the war, Dr. Hallam held honorary posts as radiologist and dermatologist at the Royal Infirmary. With the onset of war in 1914, he was engaged in the localisation of bullets and other fragments in wounded soldiers. This work was described in a report from the 3rd Northern General Hospital (Br Med J 1914; 2: 847) as follows: *'The surgical staff owe much to Major Rupert Hallam for the excellent work he has done in localising bullets and pieces of shell, and so rendering their removal in most cases a comparatively easy task'.* The report went on to include an illustrated description by Major Hallam of the technique used, a modification of the Mackenzie Davidson cross thread localisation:

'Each case is first examined with the fluorescent screen. If a bullet or fragment of shell is seen, a skiagram (a radiograph) is taken and sent to the medical officer in charge of the case. Should it be deemed advisable to remove the foreign body, stereoscopic X-ray plates are made, or the foreign body is localised; that is, its depth is calculated from a certain landmark on the skin. It will be remembered that the ordinary X-ray negative gives no idea of the contour of the limb'. After the war, Dr. Hallam returned to civilian practice. From 1928, he devoted his career to the full time practice of dermatology and earned a national and international reputation in this speciality.

Dr William Harwood Nutt and Radiation Injuries

Dr Harwood Nutt in military uniform in WW1

Records during the period of WW1 show that Dr. Harwood Nutt, who carried the rank of Captain, had clinical duties at Wharncliffe War Hospital, the Sheffield Union Workhouse, Chesterfield and Mexborough in addition to the Royal Hospital. At Wharncliffe War Hospital, Dr. Harwood Nutt was required to work largely on his own apart from assistance from 'an attendant' from the Post Mortem room. He first reported radiation dermatitis of his hands and face in 1915. His clinical work through the period of WW1 included the detection and localisation of bullets and shrapnel in a large number of wounded soldiers involving heavy doses of radiation. This undoubtedly accounted for his symptoms. The risks of radiation were recognised at the time but stringent radiation protection measures were not introduced until later. It is interesting to note the following comment in the Medical Administrator's report to the Board of Wharncliffe War Hospital dated 14th April 1916: *'Most excellent work is being carried out in the X-ray room by Captain Nutt. This work has been recognised by the Rontgen Society, and has been brought before the War Office. It deals with the protection of workers in X-rays'.*

Dr. Harwood Nutt carried on working as a radiologist until 1922 when a low white cell count was found raising concern that he might be developing aplastic anaemia. He was forced to resign because of ill-health and it is ironic that this resulted from a radiation induced illness despite his awareness of the dangers of X-rays and his attempts to introduce safety measures. He received only a small 'grant' from the War Office in recognition of this and he subsequently moved to Norwich to work as a GP until retirement. Fortunately, the earlier radiation induced illness did not compromise his longevity.

Dr. John Grout MC, CBE

Dr. J. L A. Grout

Dr. Grout was a well known Sheffield Radiologist. He worked at the Royal Hospital and at Chesterfield Royal Infirmary from 1926 to 1954. As a newly qualified doctor he joined the RAMC in 1913 and served in France and Italy in the 13th Field Ambulance. He ended the war with the rank of major, and was awarded the Military Cross. The citation read as follows: 'For conspicuous gallantry and devotion to duty in conducting a number of stretcher squads through very heavy shell fire to the aid-posts after they had previously failed to get through. Two bearers were killed and three wounded, but by his gallant action over forty stretcher cases were got to safety. Later, he personally conducted squads to these aid posts under similar circumstances'. In his career as a radiologist, Dr. Grout earned a reputation as a strong leader and disciplinarian. Radiology as a speciality was still developing and Dr. Grout campaigned locally and nationally for its recognition and advancement. There is no doubt that the lessons he learned close to the battlefield in WW1 shaped his resolve in later life and resulted in an outstanding career in radiology which was later recognised by the award of a CBE.

Conclusion

Lessons learned during the early application of X-Rays in the clinical management of wounded soldiers were applied to civilian medicine which aided the acceptance and development of the new speciality of radiology. Experience gained in organisation and leadership in the military was also put to use in establishing the new X-Ray departments.

Michael Collins

HEARTY GREETINGS
and Best Wishes for a
MERRY CHRISTMAS
and a Happy and Victorious
New Year
from the 1/3 W. Riding Field Amb.

Christmas Card designed and drawn by
W. F. Northend

William Brooks

William Brooks was born in Sheffield in 1884. He joined the Territorial Army in 1910, serving in the 3rd WRFA and was quickly promoted to Staff Sergeant. He was awarded the French Medaille Militaire for bravery having rescued two French soldiers from the battlefield and brought them back to safety, although he himself was wounded. He is caricatured below in the 'Lead Swinger' after becoming the unit's Sergeant Major.

SGT. MAJ. W. BROOKS MED MIL.
"TO BE GOOD IS NOBLE BUT TO TEACH OTHERS TO BE GOOD IS MORE NOBLE AND LESS TROUBLE."
Mark Twain.

He tragically died of his injuries on Armistice Day, 1918, his wife being told that he had a secondary pneumonia. However, his records stated that he in fact died the following day from influenza. Whether this was due to official reluctance to recognise deaths occurring on Armistice Day is difficult to know. He left a wife and five very young children and is buried in East Cambria Cemetery in France which was very close to the 22nd Clearing Station which was the last clearing station before returning home. He, like so many medics, was the first on the scene to see the devastation that man does to man.

Geoffrey Travis

World War One and its impact on the Sheffield Medical School

The original medical school was established in 1828 and was preceded for a few years by two private Schools of Anatomy in the town. The establishment of the University in 1905 led to the incorporation of the Medical School into the North Wing of its new buildings on Western Bank. Thus, at the start of the First World War in 1914, barely nine years since its formation, the Faculty of Medicine, relatively small and newly established, was thrown into the administrative turmoil of coping with a staff and student population whose number altered according to the demands of the war. This is demonstrated by examination of the Minutes of Faculty meetings held during the period 1914 to 1919. Early in September 1914, temporary arrangements were made for absence of staff and laboratory assistants, while anatomy demonstrators had joined the Royal Army Medical Corps. The Officers' Training Corps (OTC) asked medical students to attend drill practice and the Dean closed classes one morning each week for this purpose; the students to make up lost time.

In autumn 1914, it was noted that six senior students had volunteered for Red Cross work in France, Messrs, Gamm, Hill, Rae, Sharrard, Ward and Wiseman. Six months later, Hill and Ward volunteered as Probationer Surgeons in the Royal Naval Volunteer Reserve for a period of six months. In April 1915, the War Office wrote stating that War Hospitals under military control would accept 4th and 5th year students as Dressers and they would undertake the duties of Army Surgeons. The Dean agreed with this proposal. In the same month, Dr. F. Fitzwilliam Gwynne was the first Sheffield doctor to be honoured with the award of the Military Cross. He wrote to the Dean, having received a letter of congratulations from the Medical School, thanking the Faculty for their good wishes on his award. He had graduated in 1911 and was killed in action in Flanders in July 1915, three months after his award. The facsimile letter is contained in the Faculty Minutes Book.

In October 1915, the Dean reported that *'despite the calls of Military duties on the time of the staff, the department has continued to work without interruption'*. By November 1915, it is reported that the war has taken a heavy toll of the medical graduates of the University. A month later, Faculty resolved that *'1st and 2nd year men students have a duty to put themselves at the disposal of His Majesty's Government'*.

In April 1916 the Central Medical War Committee wrote to all Deans of medical schools concerned to know the number of prospective successful candidates in forthcoming Finals Examinations. In the same month, the department of Pathology took over the diagnostic work of Venereal Diseases at the request of local government. Dr. Arthur Hall was appointed Professor of Medicine. In August, 1916, a further four members of staff were mentioned in dispatches and Captain W. B. Allen, RAMC, who graduated in 1914 was awarded the Military Cross for gallantry and on October 17th, 1917, the Victoria Cross for most conspicuous gallantry and devotion to duty. He also received a Bar to his Military Cross.

In January, 1918, due to the war work and depletion of staff, the Dean was instructed to postpone the Diploma in Public Health course. In March 1918, a letter from the Ministry of National Service called on all students who had passed 2nd MB to volunteer for six months service as Probationer Surgeons in the Royal Navy. It was further reported that two students Twigg and Mathews had been wounded and R. Hawksworth and G. Milne had been discharged from the Army disabled by wounds and had returned to their studies. Three junior students had joined the Royal Navy Sick Berth Reserve and 17 students had resumed their studies after demobilisation. In addition, 18 demobilised men had joined the Faculty. In February 1919, the Faculty made recommendations for returning students to take up their courses. A year later the Conjoint Board in London enquired about attendances at lectures in clinical subjects during the War. The Dean replied that attendances had not fallen off and generally lectures were being given.

Awards as recorded in Faculty Minutes

The following members of staff have been mentioned in dispatches:
Surgeon Major Cuff, RAMC, TF.
Major E. F. Finch, RAMC, TF. 3rd West Riding Field Ambulance
Capt. J. P. Mathews, RAMC, TF.   ″   ″   ″   ″
Capt. W. B. Allen, RAMC, TF. Attached temporarily to Royal Field Artillery awarded the Military Cross for the following acts of Gallantry, 'On 14th and 20th August 1916, unhesitatingly passed through heavy German shellfire to attend two wounded men, on the second occasion working for half an hour in a wrecked dug-out at imminent risk of being buried'. He was wounded at the same time. Captain Allen graduated in 1914, He was the second medical graduate to be awarded this coveted award. Having returned to France after recovering from his wounds of August 1916, he was awarded the Victoria Cross for most conspicuous bravery and devotion to duty in October 1916. Capt. Allen, after recovering from his injuries, returned to duties in France, was again wounded and gassed in July 1917, and for the second time has been honoured by the award of a Bar to the Military Cross.
Lt-Col Brian Watts, RAMC, had been awarded the DSO for extricating a train-load of wounded from shell fire.
Surgeon Frederick G. E. Hill, R.N., was awarded the DSO for gallant conduct on one of HM Gunboats on the Tigris which is described thus: 'Finding a man on the battery deck he gallantly, under heavy fire carried him to the sick bay to dress his wounds. Whilst doing this the man received another wound through his throat and Surgeon Hill himself received a nasty wound himself to his forearm. Although in considerable pain and until his arm became too stiff to use, he proceeded to dress and tend all the wounded on board'.
Lt Col C. O. Pye-Smith, MC, DSO, RAMC had received a Bar to the DSO and since

then has been mentioned in dispatches.

Capt F. Gamm, MB, RAMC, had received the Military Cross

Capt G. K. E. Inman, MB, RAMC, had received the Military Cross.

Major A. E. Barnes, MB, RAMC, had been decorated with the Serbia Order of S.Save.

Lt Col G. H. L. Hammerton, DSO, RAMC, had been made a Companion of the Order of St Michael and St. George.

Awards 1918, as recorded in Faculty Minutes.

Lt M. G. Pettigrew, RAMC, received the Military Cross.

Lt Col G. H. L. Hammerton, mentioned in dispatches for the second time.

Major D. G. Newton, RAMC, had received the Territorial Decoration.

Major W. B. Allen, VC, MC,RAMC, awarded the DSO.

Major Fredk Gamm, MC, RAMC, Bar to Military Cross.

Capt Kingsley Inman, MC, Bar to Military Cross.

Lt Col Sinclair White, MD, MCh.,FRCS, awarded CBE.

Capt C. W. Smith, MB, FRCS, RAMC, awarded OBE.

Miss Lydia Henry, MB, awarded Croix de Guerre.

R. V. Favell, RAMC, mentioned in dispatches.

Obituaries. as recorded in Faculty Minutes

John Fitzgerald Gwynne, elder son of the late Dr C. N. Gwynne of Sheffield (a former lecturer in the School of Medicine) was a scholar in 1906, Kaye Scholar in 1909 and graduated MB in June 1911. After graduation he held various resident posts at the Sheffield Royal Infirmary and elsewhere and was gazetted Lieutenant in the RAMC in January 1914. At the outbreak of war he was sent to France. On February 19th, 1915 his name appeared on the first list of recipients of the Military Cross for distinguished bravery in action. He never saw the trophy he had so gallantly won, being killed in action in July, 1915.

Derwent Christopher Turnbull, graduated June, 1914. Soon after the outbreak of war he joined the RAMC as Temporary Lieutenant and was sent to France. Early in March 1915 whilst making an exceptionally brave attempt to carry back a wounded comrade under heavy fire, he was himself mortally wounded and died in France on 14th March, 1915.

Lt Col John Wilfred Stokes, RAMC, commanding the 3rd West Riding Field Ambulance at outbreak of war, was invalided home from the Western Front suffering from shell-shock, the effects of which led to his death. He was for a number of years a valued member of staff as an honorary demonstrator in Anatomy and an Anaesthetist at the Royal Infirmary.

2nd Lt Charles Henry Godwin joined the City Battalion at its formation, and obtaining a commission, was transferred to another regiment. He was killed in the Great Advance. He was a first year student in the Faculty, son of the late Dr, Godwin of Clowne, nr Chesterfield.

Pte Robert Bruce Mathews joined the OTC at the outbreak of war and was transferred to the City Battalion on its formation in autumn 1914. He was killed whilst succouring a comrade buried during a bombardment of the trenches on 16th May. He was the second son of Dr R. H. Mathews of this City and obtained the Medical Scholarship in 1914.

Lt Charles Cecil W. Mays, RAMC, is reported missing believed drowned, and has gone down with the torpedoed vessel on which he was proceeding in the discharge of his duties.

Capt Frank Cecil Harris was killed in action, March 1918.

The following students have laid down their lives in the service of their country;

2nd Lt C. H. Goodwin.

2nd Lt V. H. Wiseman.

2nd Lt John Stead.

Pte P. M. West.

We can but admire and pay our respects to those of our forebears who gave their lives at home and abroad in the service of their country and to admire the manner in which those who remained at home maintained the integrity of the Medical School throughout such troubled times.

James Burton

The Story of Robert Martin – when medical history was created and subsequently forgotten

The history of cardiac surgery as reported in contemporary textbooks is essentially a list of dates marking medical consensus statements, medical experience and medical achievements that made safe surgery on the heart possible. These include :

1846 General anaesthesia – William Morton in Boston.

1867 Development of antisepsis –– Robert Lister in Edinburgh.

1890 Professor Theodor Billroth – famous 19th century German Surgeon states – '*A surgeon who tries to suture a heart wound deserves to lose the esteem of his colleagues*'.

1893 Daniel Hale, Afro-American Surgeon, Closure of Laceration to Pericardium – Chicago.

July 1896 Stephen Paget in Textbook called Surgery of the Chest – '*Surgery of the heart has probably reached the limits set by nature, no new methods and no new discovery can overcome the natural difficulties that attend a wound of the heart*'.

September 1896 Ludwig Rehn, German Surgeon becomes first to suture laceration in right ventricle – patient survives.

1911-13 Transoral Endotracheal intubation and mechanical ventilation.

May 1925, Closed Mitral Valvotomy to treat Rheumatic Mitral Stenosis - Henry Souttar, London.

1928 Discovery of Antibiotics – Alexander Fleming.

1943-45 Dwight Harken, US Army Surgeon, removes more than 100 projectiles from heart and great vessels – London.

May 1953 John Gibbon performs first operation with the aid of a heart lung machine (cardiopulmonary bypass) Philadelphia.

1960s Development of Heart Valve (Ross, Starr) and Coronary Surgery (Favoloro).

In September 2011, I was speaking to the Ecclesall Parish Theatre Company in Sheffield on the 'History of Heart Surgery'. At the end of my talk, Sheila Hobson, approached me and told me a story that left me incredulous. Her great uncle, Robert Martin, a British soldier had undergone heart surgery in Malta to have a bullet removed from his heart during the 1914-18 War. Despite my incredulity, I had to investigate further and this is what I discovered.

Robert Hugh Martin was 17 years of age. He lived in Totley, and had left school as a boy to work in an office at Cole Brothers, Sheffield, later to become a John Lewis department store. More recently he had enrolled as a printer's apprentice. On his way to work one day, a woman with a white feather approached him. It was the autumn of 1914. Britain was in a state of war with Germany and Lord Kitchener was exhorting all men of 18 and above to join up. The white feather signified cowardice

46

and he clearly was mistaken for a man of 18 or older. The experience unnerved him. He decided to lie about his age and within a few days had enlisted to join the Derbyshire Yeomanry which served as both a cavalry as well as a dismounted infantry regiment. After mobilization, the regiment was moved to Egypt in 1915 and served in the ill-fated Gallipoli Campaign. The regiment was then transferred to Greece in 1916, to fight on the Salonika or Macedonian Front.

Robert Hugh Martin 1896-1918

On his 21st birthday, November 14th, 1917, Robert Martin set out on a mounted sortie. The unit came under fire from Bulgarian troops and he was hit in the chest. Unlike bullets used in modern warfare, the bullet that hit Robert was a low velocity missile. A similar injury sustained today would almost certainly have been instantly fatal. Robert Martin not only survived the impact of the bullet but also was able to ride his horse back to base before he collapsed. Physical examination and a chest X-ray revealed that the bullet had hit and traversed his right arm missing the humerus. It entered the right side of the chest between the 4th and 5th ribs and settled in the region of the heart. The fact that the bullet moved in time with cardiac pulsations on X-ray screening suggested that it might have embedded itself in the left ventricle of the heart.

What would have happened if Robert Martin sustained a similar low velocity injury as a British soldier in Helmand Province in Afghanistan in 2014? Trooper Martin would have been evacuated within 20 minutes of injury on a well equipped and well staffed Chinook Medevac helicopter, back to the hospital at Camp Bastion. He would have received treatment to secure his airway and restore circulation with rapid infusion of fluids, blood and plasma as well as prophylactic antibiotics, and soon after arrival at hospital, he would have undergone echocardiography and CT scanning of his chest. Within 1 to 2 hours of sustaining his injury, medics would have known its exact nature and what surgical intervention was required. As Robert Martin was stabilised so quickly, he would have been able to be evacuated safely on a jet transport aeroplane back to Birmingham UK where he would have been assessed within 24-36 hours by cardiac surgeons.

It is likely that due to the risk of the metallic fragment dislodging, leaving the young man with a sizeable hole in his ventricle and inevitable death from rapid cardiac tamponade as well as the risk of the projectile embolising to the lungs from its current position in the right ventricle, surgeons would have decided to operate on him. Under general anaesthesia with intravenous sedation, opiate analgesia and muscular relaxants, as well as prophylactic antibiotics, Robert Martin would have undergone a median sternotomy, a longitudinal splitting of the sternum. He would be attached to a cardiopulmonary or heart lung bypass machine. Whilst on bypass, Robert Martin was able to survive without the function of his heart (or lungs). The heart would have been stopped, the fragment of metal removed from the right ventricle and the defect repaired primarily or with a patch of pericardium. The heart and lungs would have been restarted, and the patient separated from the heart lung machine. As a red blood cell saving suction machine was used, there would only have been a 40% chance that the patient would have required a blood transfusion. The chest would have been closed with stainless steel wires and 5 to 7 days later, Robert Martin would have been discharged home back to Totley. That is what would have happened today – but what about 100 years ago? Nowhere in contemporary textbooks of cardiac surgery is the fact that less than 20 years after Theodor Bilroth made that not so prophetic statement, British and French Army surgeons were attempting to operate on the heart – often successfully, despite the fact blood transfusion was still in its infancy and that antibiotics and the heart lung bypass machine to support heart function were just pipe dreams.

This is how Robert Martin was actually managed. Soon after collapsing, he had a chest X-ray and exploratory surgery (possibly upper laparotomy) at a Salonika field hospital. The bullet was not found and a decision was made to transfer him to Malta which was known as the 'Nurse of the Mediterranean'. British troops injured in any theatre of war around the Mediterranean who required higher or convalescent care were transferred to Malta, which, smaller than the Isle of White and with a native population of less than 300,000, had 29 hospitals. The transfer from Salonika to Malta on a troopship lasted 2 months. On arrival in the Grand Harbour, Robert was transferred to St. Elmo hospital. One of the handlers transferring him to the waiting ambulance was an old friend from Totley. Robert told his mother in a letter home that he was greeted with the words 'It's a long way from Totley, eh Bob!'

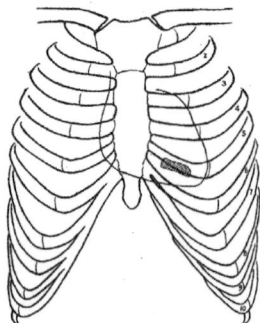

Diagram by Captain Crowe RAMC of position of Bullet

St. Elmo Hospital was where elective surgery was carried out in Malta. It had an excellent reputation with hundreds of procedures having been carried out with a zero mortality rate. Robert Martin was observed for a few days. When he complained of palpitations associated with a very rapid pulse rate, a decision was made to attempt surgical removal of the bullet that was embedded in his heart. The operation took place on February 16th, 1918. The surgeons were Colonel Sir Charles Ballance, a British Army doctor and Dr. Marguerite White, an American volunteer surgeon. Lieutenant-Colonel Shirley was the Anaesthetist.

Sir Charles Ballance was by training an ENT and Otoneurological surgeon who had worked at St. Thomas's Hospital and the National Hospital for Paralysed and Epileptics in Queen's Square, Bloomsbury (now known as the National Hospital for Neurology and Neurosurgery). On this occasion, he was, with Sir Charles Symonds, one of the senior military surgeons organizing surgical services in Malta.

The heart was exposed through a Kocher's incision, a left sided anterolateral thoracotomy that necessitated the removal of the 4th, 5th and sixth costal cartilages. As the left internal mammary artery crossed the operative field, it was ligated and divided. The edge of the left pleura was seen and opening of the left pleural cavity was avoided. This was significant as it meant the patient could breath spontaneously throughout the procedure without the aid of endotracheal intubation and mechanical ventilation. Although the surgical technique is documented in some detail, the actual anaesthetic technique used was not. The surgeon palpated the heart and was able to accurately locate the bullet. Using 2 purse string sutures, and great skill he was able to cut open the heart, extirpate the bullet and close the resulting hole in one deft movement, thus limiting the blood loss to less than 500 mls. The wound was closed and the patient woken up. Robert Martin had survived and the operation deemed a success.

During the first few days after surgery, the patient did well and appeared to be making a good recovery. On day 3, it was clear however that Robert Martin had developed what surgeons of the day most feared – a serious wound infection. Infections of wounds sustained in military conflict are still common today, bullets and shrapnel being no less filthy than they were 100 years ago. What has transformed outcomes is the management of infected wounds – laying them open and application of negative pressure dressings together with antibiotic therapy. Sadly for Robert Martin such devices and drugs were not available to physicians in 1917. The wound was reopened and the pericardial cavity was irrigated with saline. Ether was administered subcutaneously and mustard applied to the extremities to treat low blood pressure. As laboratory tests suggested the patient was anaemic, undoubtedly due to bone marrow suppression, which occurs in patients who are septic, it was decided to perform a blood transfusion. In 1917, blood banks did not exist. Blood transfusion was in its infancy and carried considerable risks for both donor and recipient. A fit soldier with matching blood group was identified. He underwent a surgical procedure to expose and isolate his radial artery. This was divided and the donor soldier bled into a bottle containing an anticoagulant drug. The blood in the bottle was then infused into the ill patient. Sadly despite this and other attempted treatments, Robert Martin succumbed to the wound infection and resulting mediastinitis (infection of the deep organ space around the heart and other organs). He died on March 14th, 1917. A detailed postmortem examination confirmed the presence of staphylococcal mediastinitis that had spread along multiple tissue planes.

Robert Martin is buried in one of the Commonwealth Military Cemeteries on the island of Malta. Details of the treatment of Robert Martin and other soldiers with similar injuries, some of whom survived are documented in great detail in articles and talks published between 1918 and 1922. Despite the fact that these cases have been archived in great detail, they have inexplicably disappeared from the history chapters of contemporary textbooks of Cardiothoracic Surgery. The heroic efforts of Ballance, White and other military surgeons as well as the sacrifice of Robert Martin contributed to our body of knowledge that made cardiac surgery possible and safe.

It is only right that in this year marking the centenary of the start of a conflagration that changed societies and killed millions that the story of Robert Martin is remembered.

Norman Briffa

Anaesthesia in the Great War

Though nitrous oxide or 'laughing gas' had been used for tooth extraction in 1844, it was too weak for major surgery. In October 1846 in Boston, USA, William Morton was the first to publicly anaesthetise a patient with ether allowing pain free surgery. It was rapidly taken up in Great Britain, but in Scotland, James Simpson introduced chloroform a year later. Easier to administer and pleasanter for the patient it became popular, though there were objections to its use in childbirth. These ended after John Snow gave chloroform to Queen Victoria during the birth of her seventh child in 1853. Antisepsis, introduced by Lister in 1865, necessitated lengthy preoperative preparation which was difficult with unanaesthetised patients. In 1868, nitrous oxide was reintroduced, compressed in cylinders. It was useful for short minor operations and for dental extractions.

Before the beginning of the 20th century only a few doctors, mostly in London, specialised in anaesthesia. Elsewhere anaesthetics were given by a variety of hospital workers; from housemen/interns, dentists, medical students, nurses and porters. However, before the Great War, increased numbers of operations indicated the need for doctors who specialised in administering anaesthetics. In Sheffield, according to a graph in the 1912 Annual Report of the Royal Infirmary, the number of operations had risen by 50% between 1901 and 1906 (from 1,100 to 1,800). There is no similar Royal Hospital graph but a new ether apparatus had been ordered in January 1901 and Mr. Herbert Hallam was appointed an Honorary Anaesthetist in November 1902. In 1904, Mr. Henry Temple Wightman seems to be the Infirmary's first Honorary Anaesthetist but Mr. Alfred Reckless may have preceded him. Wightman was soon followed by Mr. J.W. Stokes and Dr. Rupert Hallam. By mid-1905, the Royal Hospital had established two more Honorary Anaesthetists; Mr. Norton Milner and Dr. C. Graham Murray. Honorary Anaesthetists were local general practitioners who attended usually for one 3 hour session per week and were paid an honorarium of £25 p.a. They were re-elected to their posts annually.

In 1911, W. Dakin Mart & R. Vernon Favell (who replaced Rupert Hallam) were added to the Infirmary's Hon. Anaesthetists. In May 1913, the Royal Hospital *'resolved that four Anaesthetists be appointed'* and in November *'another anaesthetist be appointed'*. Favell had moved to the Royal Hospital & R. G. Abercrombie was also appointed making five. M.W. Sneddon replaced Favell at the Infirmary in 1913 but he had vacated the post by 1915. In April 1919; *'Dr. Sneddon has returned from the war'*. Wightman resigned and retired from practice in 1914; he was replaced by T. Robertson. On 3rd March 1915, Dakin Mart wrote to the Board to resign; he had been called for Military duties from *'Monday last'*. Mr H. Caiger FRCS was made temporary anaesthetist on 19th May. He and Robertson paid £50 p.a. from 1st May, and it is likely they had two sessions.

Returning to the Royal Hospital, in a letter dated 22nd September 1914, R. G. Abercrombie resigned: *'withdrawing from the post...accepted for active service'*. However, it appears he continued at least until 1917 when he became an 'Assistant Physician'. He had been a Civil Surgeon to H.M. Forces in South Africa. He sailed there in May 1902 and took local discharge in 1904/5; he was awarded the South African Medal with four clasps (information kindly supplied by Capt Pete Starling of the Army Medical Museum). Mr. J. B. H Holroyd and Mr. J. H. Wylie were appointed in November 1914 'until after War in place of Dr Abercrombie and Mr Vernon Favell'. Before this, in January 1911, Holroyd had provided anaesthesia at Fir Vale/NGH, and in November 1913 he had been appointed 'anaesthetist to the Dental Dept', a busy part of the Royal, evidently. Holroyd had been Casualty Officer at the Royal Hospital from 25th July, 1910. In May 1915 Dr Vernon Mossman replaced Holroyd as 'temporary Dental anaesthetist'. Mr. A. H. H. Howard became temporary anaesthetist in April 1916 but in August his resignation was accepted and he was replaced by Mossman. Around this time the Dental Department was closed and the premises taken over by the Military Authorities.

The Proceedings of the Royal Infirmary Board has a newspaper cutting dated 1st March 1916: an advertisement for *'two anaesthetists to be appointed for the period of the war but candidates must be ineligible for Service with HM Forces'*. At the same date Mr. Alfred Reckless be *'appointed Hon. Consulting Anaesthetist...for valuable services gratuitously rendered in a time of stress during the Great War'*. Three more anaesthetists were appointed for the period of the war on 15th March at £25 p.a. Mr. C. F. Coombe, Dr. Norton Milner and Dr. J. H. Wilks. In the Medical Directory of 1916 Milner was Capt RAMC, 3rd Northern General Hospital. There is no mention of his resignation at the Royal Hospital but he does not appear on the list of honoraria paid after December 1915. In June it was decided to engage an additional anaesthetist to the Honorary Ophthalmic Surgeon *'for the period of the War'* and Mr. Simon Ryan FRCS (Ed.) was appointed in July. After this there is no mention of anaesthetists until 1919, when Dr. Coombe retired from his temporary war time appointment following the return of Dr. Sneddon. At the Royal Hospital Holroyd was called for Military Duty on 31st March 1917. Soon after, Dr. H. G. Dickinson was appointed temporary anaesthetist in his place. R. E. Pleasance became Hon. Anaesthetist in September 1918. Subsequently, in 1932, he was one of the first members of the Association of Anaesthetists of Great Britain & Ireland and in 1948 one of the first Fellows of the Faculty of Anaesthetists of the Royal College of Surgeons.

Such was the scale of casualties in the War that there was an enormous demand for anaesthesia. Any doctor could be called upon to give an anaesthetic and many who gave them had very little training or experience. At least four Sheffield anaesthetists were called up for military service and it is notable that the importance of appointing experienced doctors, ineligible for H.M. Forces, to provide anaesthesia was emphasised by the Royal Infirmary's advert mentioned above.

Ether, chloroform, ethyl chloride and nitrous oxide were used for general anaesthesia in the Great War. The first two were needed in such vast amounts that special facilities were granted to the manufacturers to increase their output. Both were simply dripped on to the Schimmelbusch mask often by non-medically trained staff. Clover's ether inhaler and Buxton's modification of the Junker apparatus for chloroform were sophisticated pieces of equipment allowing controlled vaporisation. Steel was needed for munitions, so nitrous oxide and oxygen in cylinders were necessarily less available. The British Oxygen Company provided oxygen while French firms filled nitrous oxide cylinders. By 1916, a nitrous oxide/oxygen machine was available; based on equipment devised by the American anaesthetist, James Gwathmey, it was first modified by Geoffrey Marshall and then by H. E. G. Boyle. It was used with or without local anaesthetic infiltration for short operations. A warm ether vaporiser designed by Dr. (later Sir) Francis Shipway though elaborate, provided better surgical conditions, improved recovery and less pollution. From early 1916 it was in regular use at Casualty Clearing Stations. Chloroform was used less often because of its hypotensive effect and the occurrence of sporadic cardiac arrest. Ethyl chloride was seldom used in contrast to French and German anaesthetic practice.

As mentioned above local anaesthesia was used; commonly Novocaine (procaine) and Stovaine (named after its discoverer; M. Fourneau (which is French for stove). Cocaine, the first local anaesthetic discovered, was only applied topically because of its toxic and addictive properties. Procaine/Novocaine was a very weak local anaesthetic improved by the addition of adrenaline and mainly employed for infiltration. Since Stovaine caused sloughing of the skin it was used as a spinal anaesthetic in a 5 % glucose solution. Because spinal anaesthesia causes hypotension it was dangerous when used in exsanguinated casualties so the technique was abandoned except for lower limb amputations.

General anaesthesia in the French Army was by ethyl chloride or a mixture of ether and chloroform employing the Ombrédanne apparatus. This was a sophisticated vaporiser that remained in use in Europe well into the second half of the 20th century. However, inhalational anaesthesia was dangerous for gassed patients and for those in shock. Spinal anaesthesia using Stovaine was useful but caused hypotension and so was contraindicated in patients with severe blood loss. Richet favoured the use of rectal chloralose and used it intravenously in 1918. By the end of the war it was accepted that the anaesthetist was no longer an auxiliary but essential as the surgeon's own assistant.

There is no doubt that *'the art of administering anaesthesia was greatly developed during the war…' Chapter IX: Anaesthesia. In: Official History of the Medical Services in the Great War by H. P. Crampton.*

Adrian Padfield

VOL. II—NO. 7

Drawing by W. F. Northend in the 'Lead Swinger' of the 3rd West Riding Field Ambulance, possibly at Essex Farm

Wounded and home to Blighty

World War One was one of the bloodiest wars in human history. During the war the Royal Army Medical Corps (RAMC) dealt with 5½ million casualties (from battle and disease). 3% died, 55% returned to service; 58% of battle casualties were due to shrapnel – this was an artillery war – which caused shredding wounds with clothing and blood and tissue fluid intermixed, which became gangrenous in an era before antibiotics. Other casualties included those suffering from mental illness or shell shock and there were 186,000 admissions from gassing (mainly chlorine, later phosgene and mustard gas) of whom 5,900 died, representing 10% of total wounded. Other diseases, such as dysentery, also flourished in unhygienic conditions and the influenza epidemic of 1918 also claimed many lives.

Ambulance trains were first used during the First World War in France and Belgium to transport wounded or sick soldiers to hospital. They were also called first aid trains, hospital trains, casualty evacuation trains or travelling hospitals and were specifically designed so that nurses of the British Red Cross and the Queen Alexandra's Imperial Military Nursing Service (QAIMNS) and army medical officer doctors and orderlies of the RAMC could continue the care of evacuated soldiers.

Early History

While the Crimean War is possibly best remembered by the work of Florence Nightingale it was also notable for the first use of railways to transport wounded soldiers from the battlefield. William Russell, a no-holds-barred war correspondent for The Times, wrote in 1854 *'Four wagons filled with sick and wounded soldiers, ran from headquarters to town in less than half an hour. The men were propped up on their knapsacks and seemed very comfortable. What a change from the ghastly processions one met with some weeks ago, formed of dead and dying men, hanging from half-starved horses or dangling about on French mule-litters'*. This is probably the earliest description of what could be termed ambulance trains.

Rail transport of the wounded was also a feature of the American Civil War. According to one contemporary source in 1862 *'The worse cases are put inside the covered cars – closed, windowless boxes – sometimes with a little straw or a blanket to lie on, oftener without. They arrive a festering mass of dead and living together'*.

The situation did improve somewhat, particularly in America, and for the Prussian and Boer Wars, towards the end of the nineteenth century; by then trains were being constructed, or more often adapted, to transport casualties.

Ambulance Trains on the Western Front

Given this earlier history it seems quite remarkable therefore that none of the putative combatants for World War 1 had a strategic plan to cope with the wounded, although intricate programmes had been put in action to get the troops there in the first place! Even the Germans were woefully remiss. From Deutsche Medizinische Wochenschrift – *'In the early part of November 1914 soldiers who had lain for days in trenches half full of water, and who had been exposed also to night frosts, were dispatched on long railway journeys in dirty trucks, a many as 30 men, probably suffering from dysentery, lying on a little straw, packed like sardines, without attention or protection from the cold'.*

Wounded soldiers waiting to be 'entrained'

The British started off just as badly – despite pre-war discussions between the railway companies and the War Railway Council arguments over costs meant that, at the start of war, there were six ambulance train detachments of 45 men with two officers, with no trains ready for them! It had been assumed the movement of British casualties from the front line to the French ports would be made using the French 'trains sanitaires'. Instead, they were initially given a hundred goods wagons and a few passenger coaches by the French – to be improvised into basic ambulance trains. The wagons were disinfected and stretcher cases laid on clean straw, but conditions were no better, and probably worse, than those afforded to soldiers in earlier wars. Thus experiences of these trains were not pleasant – they were windowless, often

Interior of an ambulance train

overloaded and could fall off the tracks. They smelt with infected wounds and soil and straw of the battle field and sanitary arrangements were poor. Patients could be incontinent. Buckets of urine and faeces would be tipped from the moving train, trying to avoid French sentries and line-side railway workers – giving new meaning to the phrase 'garde l'eau'. Gassed patients had the gas condensed into their clothing adding to the smell. Everyone smoked which mitigated the stench. Ambulance trains were slow – 12 miles an hour was a good travelling speed – as they had to compete with other trains going up to the front with fresh troops and ammunition.

'A train of cattle trucks came in from Rouen with all the wounded as they were picked up without a spot of dressing on any of their wounds, which were septic and full of straw and dirt. ... a twenty hours' journey with them in frightful smells and dirt ... they'd been travelling already for two days'.

'... the stench of the wounds was nauseating and none were more conscious of it than the sufferers themselves'.

'My next lucid moment came later when I found I was on the top bunk of a carriage in an ambulance train... I know that whoever was on the bunk above me died during the journey, and there was a horrible smell around me that seemed to get worse all the time'.

Within a couple of months a fleet of ambulance trains was assembled by the British and French – initially a motley collection of coaches from different companies with incompatible lighting and braking systems, and frequently supplied by whatever medical equipment and drugs that could be bought or commandeered en route. Subsequently the first purpose, British-built 'khaki' trains (eventually 30 in number, several built with voluntary contributions) arrived in France, to supplement the 11 French trains, so that by the end of 1914 an effective service was being established. The RAMC provided medical and ancillary support. The ever-increasing nursing presence was mostly from the QAIMNS – known affectionately as QAs – and the British Red Cross. The QAs were distinguishable from other nurses by the short scarlet capes they wore. It is from the nurses (often from middle or upper class backgrounds) that we get most of our information on what life was really like on the ambulance trains. First hand accounts from the casualties themselves are fewer – many

A nurse dressing a wound

men were too ill, or too sedated, to remember their experience; the more fortunate sitting wounded were far too occupied dreaming of getting home to 'Blighty' to think about recording their experience. Edward Addison, a Canadian soldier, said *'he had never had such an awful time in his life'*. On the other hand Sir Oliver Lyle, then a captain in the Highland Light Infantry, recalls that *'The restful feeling in that vile train was wonderful. One knew that for a few weeks at least one would not hear a bloody gun again. It was an extraordinary relief.'* Joseph Pickard, stretcher bearer in 1916, was himself badly wounded in the back and abdomen – his bumpy and seemingly interminable journey on the top bunk of the three-berth Khaki train proved agonising, despite morphine, and humiliating because of his leaky perforated bladder.

Another source of information is from the memoirs of the Quaker men (often conscientious objectors) who served as part of the Friends Ambulance Unit, comprising four trains – like all other ambulance trains each was its own community and the Friends, in particular, were good at keeping up morale; they even had their own regular newsletters, with jokes and articles on local natural history and other non-military topics

'I think they thought that we had a pretty filthy job you see. I don't remember any hostility at all and of course, we used to go to estaminets and things in villages and drink with the troops and I think that there was no feeling that we were dodgers or anything like that'.

From the personal testimonies of ambulance train staff it seems that the authority structure was minimal, the nursing work generalist (as much about maintaining morale as dressing wounds) and there was a close identification with the train and fellow crew members. Later in the war German POWs were also carried on the trains – from contemporary records there was genuine sympathy from both staff and British patients for these bewildered young casualties of battle.

' I felt, if I may say so, more sorry for the Germans who were badly maimed because I realised that when they got back to hospital they wouldn't have anyone to come and sympathise with them' - Pope Russell.

One typical extract, from the war diaries of QAs who served aboard hospital trains published anonymously by the Nursing Times during the Great War, reads – *'They were bleeding faster than we could cope and the agony of getting them off the stretchers on to the top bunks is a thing to forget'*.

From the memoirs of the casualties themselves

'John and Owen start off with me to battalion headquarters. John keeps patting my head and telling me not to worry and that I'll be alright. He forgets he's carrying a stretcher and they drop me off twice. I think the rum ration will be a bit short, but I am grateful to them all the same'.

'Somewhere before dark my stretcher was on flat ground in a field of stretchers, as though we were a carefully cultivated crop of some choice plant ready for harvest, waiting to be reaped. My heart leapt up when I beheld an English girl kneeling beside me, gentle hands seeking where to give me an injection – then back to unconsciousness'.

'I received with joy one of those miserable bottle things that the hospitals consider good substitutes for jerries. I started to pee into it & to my dismay I found it full & overflowing. I was in the top stretcher, they are arranged in three tiers, so I looked down to see the chap underneath me gazing with a fixed stare at a wet patch above him which dripped regularly down on to him. Fortunately he was a sportsman'.

Nurses waiting to take on board the wounded

Phillip Gibbs, official reporter of the Daily Chronicle, watched as a long ambulance train pulled up near the village of Choques and quickly fill up with men suffering all kinds of wounds. The first to board were thousands of *'lightly wounded'*, he said, who *'crowded the carriages, leaned out of the windows with their bandaged heads and arms, shouting at friends they saw in the other crowds. The spirit of victory, and of lucky escape, uplifted these lads...And now they were going home to bonny Scotland, with a wound that would take some time to heal'*. Next to board were those who came on stretchers *'from which no laughter came'*. One young Londoner, *'was so smashed about the face'*, said Gibbs, *'that only his eyes were uncovered between the bandages, and they were glazed with the first film of death'*. Another young soldier *'had his jaw blown clean away. A splendid boy of the Black Watch, was but a living trunk'*, he said, *'both his arms and legs were shattered and would be one of those who go about in boxes on wheels'*. A group of blinded men *'were led to the train by wounded comrades, 'groping', very quiet, thinking of a life of darkness ahead of them…'*

Ambulance trains were a chain in the link of medical evacuation. Regimental Medical Officers patched up minor wounds and sent their patients back into battle. The more seriously wounded were given first aid then taken by motor ambulance to a casualty clearing station – a field hospital close behind the lines. These field hospitals were usually set up close to a railway line. When patients had been given emergency treatment and stabilised they were loaded into an ambulance train and transferred to a base hospital. Patient transport in wartime – motor ambulances, trains and ships – was protected under international law if properly marked. However, as train tracks were important military infrastructure and could be targeted by the enemy, working on an ambulance train could be both dangerous and uncomfortable. By the end of the war the trains were much improved with a kitchen and surgical facilities, and even flowers in old shell cases. To ensure better hygiene and the ability to scrub them down, the operating theatres would be completely tiled. Emergency operations would be performed despite the movement of the train, the cramped conditions and poor lighting. The food was poor, mainly bully beef stew and biscuits and if you had a facial injury you could starve.

Ambulance Trains in the UK

The role of ambulance trains in the United Kingdom was different from that of medical trains on the Western Front. There, patients were entrained from medical units scattered over a large area where their wounds had only received emergency treatment. On the train to the base, they received proper medical attention. This continued at the base hospital and in the hospital ships that carried them home.

Nurses with an ambulance train at Liverpool Station in 1916. This train was on display in several stations in Lancashire and Yorkshire and almost certainly in Sheffield before being taken to the Western Front. © National Railway Museum

Consequently, when they arrived at home ports most casualties were already in a reasonably stable condition. Whilst they were being carried by hospital ship to the UK and while still at sea, the ship would cable information ahead of the various categories of patients they had onboard and their estimated time of arrival at port. Each patient was labelled with details of his wound; another label was marked with one of five areas in Britain nearest his home. If a man was seriously injured a plain red label was also attached to him, indicating that he required 'special consideration.' Before disembarkation began, huge 'reception sheds on the quayside were lit and heated'. Beyond the sheds the ambulance trains waited. Early in the conflict, a group of regional railway companies donated 12 ambulance trains to the army medical services and very soon, they were carrying patients from mainly Southampton, but also Dover, to different parts of the UK. As the home-bound casualties mounted, four emergency trains made up of corridor coaches and dining cars came into service to accommodate 'sitting' patients. It is estimated that, during the war, nearly eight thousand ambulance train journeys were made carrying one and a quarter million patients!

During the war Sheffield was part of the 3rd Northern General Hospital Group. Wharncliffe War Hospital and the main civilian hospitals and various other units (smaller hospitals and schools, or other institutes, converted for the purpose) received sick and wounded soldiers. These men would arrive at one the Sheffield stations (Sheffield Victoria of the Great Central Railway or Sheffield Midland of the Midland Railway), often during the night to avoid adverse effects on public morale.

In these hospitals treatment was continued and those not badly injured or disabled were then sent back to the Western Front. Post-traumatic (war-related) stress disorders were only just being recognised as 'illnesses' at this time and some unfortunate sufferers were taken back in padded railway coach cells!

Reminiscences of Life on Ambulance Trains

These first hand recollections from staff, patients and observers derive from various secondary archived sources. Unsurprisingly, the written records are mostly from more articulate individuals with good education. So as not to alarm or demoralise the British public newspaper reports from the time were severely censored.

'But for the war I should have been reading Economics at Cambridge. I learned more about life by cleaning lavatories and tending wounded men than I should have done by attending lectures and writing essays'.

'We were the survivors, few amongst us would ever tell the truth to our friends and relations in England. We were carrying something in our heads which belonged to us alone, and to those we had left behind us in the battle' – Siegfried Sassoon 1916.

An extract from nurse Mary Stewart-Richardson's account of work on a First World War ambulance train in 1914:

After being on night duty for the inside of a week at No 3 CCS at Villeneuve Triage, I received orders on 26th Sept to proceed as Sister in Charge of No 2 Ambulance Train.

Need of sisters on ambulance trains

My experience of the conditions one received casualties in from the trains during the time I was Night Sister at the Station Workshops at Villeneuve showed one the urgent need for women nurses on the trains. No doubt the personnel then in charge had done what they could for the sufferers, but the conditions were pitiable in the extreme, of those matters which the woman nurse knows is not only comfort, but also the means of restoring vitality in giving repose to mind and body of patients suffering as those men were, who usually came straight from the battlefield to the train.

Sisters on no 2. train

I started with the Sisters detailed for my staff to find the train somewhere amongst the interminable lines at that huge railway station. My staff consisted of Sister Bulloch, S/N Susan McIntosh, and S/N Eva Schofield. Miss McCarthy saw us before starting; and told me she could give no definite outline of the work before us, but trusted to our common sense to do all possible for the patients, and to use the necessary tact in dealing with trying or difficult problems.

Opposition to sisters on trains

This last piece of advice I soon realized the value of, as, in finding the train on that hot Sept morning, (trailing down the rows of lines dragging our hand luggage,) I also found a very decided spirit of opposition to our boarding the train at all. For the Officer Commanding (OC) (whom later, I held in the highest respect and esteem, for his many excellent qualities, and able management as OC) was to say the least of it, not encouraging, and vowed there was no accommodation for us, no means of feeding us, and altogether not only would we be greatly in the way, but he considered we were wholly unnecessary as a portion of the train staff. I told him firmly that my orders were to proceed on the train with the other three Sisters, and those orders I intended to carry out. Further that we were there to be of as much use, and to give as little trouble as possible, and that those were also our firm intentions. He looked at me speechless! and then climbed into a first class compartment into which I quickly followed him, with the other Sisters, making up my mind that once I had set foot in that train, not to leave it again.

Sisters' quarters on train

He showed me an end compartment (next to the lavatory) and asked if that would accommodate all four of us. I quickly assented, inwardly feeling aghast at the prospect of four women with their hand luggage living, and sleeping in such close quarters; but the only way I felt to prove our intentions, was to accept anything offered to begin with. After a few minutes, I was told we might, during the journey up for patients, occupy another first class compartment next door; this I gratefully agreed to, privately intending it should always be Sisters' Quarters. A batman was detailed for our use, and various household requisites, brushes, basins, etc sent to us from the Stores. We were told we would be on rations, and that no cooking could be done for us except by our own batman in our own quarters.

Rations
The rations were chiefly bully beef, biscuits, jam, cheese, and cocoa which personally I did not enjoy, as in the first week I swallowed two of my own teeth with those biscuits, but bread was procurable after a week or two.

Train record
The train, improvised for ambulance use from odds and ends of French rolling stock would have been looked on with horror, even six months later, but it already had the record of having been nearer the line to fetch wounded, and brought more down the line, than any of the other ambulance trains, then alas! only numbering six in all. After hearing of its record, I understood somewhat the spirit of opposition to Sisters coming on the train. Very naturally the OC and personnel generally, thought that with women on board, they could not risk making the desperate sallies to rescue wounded which had been their ambition and glory; and I am convinced it was, the dislike to the idea of letting women in any way enter the danger zone, that had called forth such a surly welcome to us by the OC. He thought his already heavy responsibilities were being enormously increased by our presence.

No 27 Ambulance Train. The night of 10th October 1916
On the night of 10th November 1916, No.27 Ambulance Train was targeted during a long hostile bombing raid in the vicinity of Amiens railway station. As the result of their work that night, all three nursing sisters on the train, Kate Mahony, Ethel Thompson and Mabel Evans were awarded the Military Medal. The following two accounts outline the happenings that night, and how their actions resulted in their decoration for bravery. First a newspaper report of the time; source unknown but most likely from Sheffield – possibly Sheffield Daily Independent.

The alarm, screeched forth into the night air by a great Strombos horn, like a factory buzzer, reached British ambulance train No.27 as it was drawing a heavy load of wounded away from a town in the vicinity of the Somme front one autumn night. There were three British nursing sisters – Sister Kate Mahony, Sister Ethel Kate Thompson, and Sister Mabel Louise Evans – on it. The driver brought the train to a standstill. In its coaches nearly 500 wounded men, some able to walk, but most of them lying still and helpless on their train cots, awaited what the night should bring them. The first anti-aircraft gun sent forth a whistling shell. Others joined in. But the aircraft came on steadily. It was clear they had an 'object'.

'Boom' – a bomb dropped in a field. Up went a shower of earth, which came pattering down like heavy rain upon the roof of the coaches. A second bomb dropped nearer. The coaches rocked and the wounded men began to moan. Another bomb fell. It seemed to fall right on the train itself, though actually it was some yards away. Crash went every window. Out went every handlamp. The train gave a heave that threw the patients out of their beds. They rolled pell mell – they and their wounds and their splints and their beds in the middle of the coach.

And then a woman's clear voice rang out in the coach. *'Now do be quiet and good boys till I light a lamp'*. A hand struck a match and applied it to the wick of a handlamp. Sister Kate Mahony stood calm and undismayed in the entrance of the coach *'Now just wait till I get this wretched little lamp to burn and we'll have you all in bed in no time; Corporal, you come along and give me a hand,'* she added, still holding the match to the wick. And the men in that carriage say that the hand never even trembled. They lay huddled there, some in bed, some on the floor, fascinated by the sight. She got hold of orderlies by the arm. *'Here, you come and help,'* she said, and orderlies obeyed. In another coach was Sister Evans; in another Sister Thompson; both of them, like Sister Mahony, models of womanly gentleness and courage. And all this time – for a full hour the attack lasted – the sisters in white moved from coach to coach giving courage by their wonderful example and practical help.

'Man, I've seen some cool things,' said the Commandant to a representative of the Evening News, *'but the like of those women and the work they did that night I have never seen.'* And stowed somewhere in the records of the War Office is the report made on the behaviour of the three sisters – Mahony, Evans and Thompson – that night by the Commandant of the train, and it contains these words – *'Patients and staff alike felt that they had to play up to the wonderful standard set by the sisters'.*

Sister Mabel Louise Evans is a native of Sheffield, and received her training at Sheffield Royal Hospital. When war broke out she was a member of the Territorial Force Nursing Section, and immediately volunteered for foreign service. She did not, however, get sent abroad at once, but was put on the staff of the Third Northern General Hospital, subsequently receiving orders for duty at one of the base hospitals in France. After a spell at this class of work she was put on to ambulance train duty between the clearing stations and the base, and it was while she was engaged on this mission that her courage and coolness in danger won for her the rare distinction justly awarded*.

And from the service file of Ethel Kate Thompson, a copy of the letter written by the Officer Commanding, mentioned above. It is addressed to the Deputy Assistant Director of Medical Services, Ambulance Trains, and dated November 1916.

'I desire to draw attention to the courage and coolness shown by:
    Sister M. L. Evans, TFNS.*
    Sister K. Mahony, QAIMNSR.
    Sister E. K. Thompson, QAIMNSR.
    on the night of the 10th inst.

We were carrying down a full load of sick and wounded (450) and our arrival at Amiens coincided with the beginning of an aeroplane attack. All 'stood to' – electric lights were switched off and hand lamps lit etc. We ran on until halted outside the Main Station. All around the anti-aircraft guns and maxims were in hot action. Among the helpless patients and among the shell shock patients there was considerable alarm, which was increased as loud explosions began to be heard. The firing continued and the explosions crept nearer, until, for us, the climax was reached when at short intervals five bombs fell in our immediate neighbourhood, near enough to send debris over the train. Twice the lamps were blown out; windows were broken on both sides of the train. The nearest bomb tore up the off rail of the line next to us, smashed the windows and rocked the coach so much that the patients on one side were thrown out of their cots. The attack lasted an hour. The Sisters rose to the occasion from the very beginning. Carrying hand lamps they went about their jobs coolly, collectedly and cheerfully. Their influence in stopping panic and allaying alarm, was I believe, greater than that of the officers – just because they were Sisters – patients and personnel felt they had to play up to the standard set by the Sisters. They had their chance and rose to it magnificently.

W. M. Darling, Officer Commanding No.27 Ambulance Train.

*Evans. Mabel Louise, Sister. MM. For bravery at the front. Of 158 Crookesmoor Road. From Sheffield Daily Independent 26th January 1917.

Life on an Ambulance Train in 1914
by Sister M. Phillips (QAIMNS) – an account which combines the humour and stoicism which typifies the time.

The ambulance trains in 1914 were not the trains of joy and beauty which they developed into later in the war, anything that ran on wheels and could be attached to an engine was utilized in the early days of 1914. They were chiefly trains composed of wagons bearing the legend 'Hommes 40, Chevaux (en long) 8,' so that the staff of No.7 Ambulance train thought itself lucky. The front half of the train consisted of the 1st class French 'couchette' or carriages fitted with sleeping berths, so that at least the patients had a comfortable couch on which to lie; the rear half of the train simply consisted of ordinary third class railway carriages with their hard narrow wooden seats, but these were always reserved so far as possible for 'sitting cases'.
All the coaches on the train were entirely unconnected, and those nurses who have only carried out nursing duties on trains whose entire length it was possible to walk without once going outside, can hardly realize the inconvenience, sometimes amusing but at most times vexatious, to which one was put in 1914. Quite a number of teapots and cups and saucers came to an untimely end from the habit which the batman had of placing those articles on the footboard of the train when bringing the early morning tea; then, leaving them while he went back for something which he had forgotten – the train would start with a jerk – and 'goodbye-ee' to tea for that morning. The greatest inconvenience of all was the difficulty of attending to

the patients, and the vexation of spirit occasioned when you had settled up one coachful of aching weary men, by the knowledge that there were still hundreds to be attended to. Climbing from coach to coach by way of the footboard was a practice absolutely forbidden, though, like more than one other rule, it was more honoured in the breach than in the observance. Frequently this means of passing from one coach to another was an absolute necessity in the interests of the patients. No doubt a French stationmaster in a little out of the way French village will probably remember to this day the sight that met his amazed gaze in the very early hours of a beautiful September morning in 1914. An ambulance train was flying through his station with an English sister clinging like a limpet to the side of the train. She had, I remember, a moment of horror when the train dashed into the station, wondering whether the platform would be higher than the footboard; but luckily all French country platforms are very low. After the Battle of the Aisne the train was garaged for a few days in a little village called Crepy-en-Valois; while the British armies moved north. Movement of troops took place only at night, and whether the whole British Army passed through this little town, we, of course, did not know; but at least one member of the staff of the train will never forget the continuous, apparently endless, procession of men, horses and guns. The men never spoke a word, either to us or among themselves. The only noise was the low, deep rumble of the procession itself, seeming to fill the autumn night with fear and foreboding.

On the night of October 31st to November 1st, No.7 Ambulance train had the luck, or ill-luck, to be on Ypres station – the date that marks the beginning of the wonderful first Battle of Ypres. The train received its baptism of fire that night – poor train – it could not have run away had it wanted to; the engine had returned down the line for water. A neighbouring improvised train loaded with minor wounded had better luck and secured an engine from somewhere, and, as it pulled out of the station into safety, I expect poor old No.7 heaved a small sigh of envy, although I like to think that even had a second engine been handy, No.7 would have stuck to her post; but with what feelings of great thankfulness and relief she hooked herself on to her engine the next morning, and gave him a graphic description of those horrid shells which had made holes in her sides and broken her windows, while he was away at Hazebrouck imbibing water.

After the establishment of Casualty Clearing Stations the work on ambulance trains was not nearly so arduous. In the first days patients were entrained with all the dirt, mud, and blood of battle on them. All were fully dressed. Many had not had their boots off their feet for five or six weeks. Only those who have experienced it, know what it means to undress a heavy man, badly wounded and lying on the narrow seat of a railway carriage. Never before had it been brought home to me what a quantity of clothes a man wears. On many an occasion it has seemed a task worthy of a Hercules, but when the deed was done, the man undressed and in soft dry pyjamas, even though maybe there had only been time to sponge his face, hands, and feet – then indeed labour had its reward – the gratitude, the patience, the infinite endurance of the men was a constant marvel to behold. One felt that the utmost one could do was but a drop in the ocean of their discomfort, and their gratitude for that drop was sometimes more than one could bear. When the Casualty Clearing Stations were established the men came on board washed, fed, and in pyjamas; so that we did not have to begin on the bedrock of things as it were, but had only to carry on the good work already commenced. It was with very mingled feelings that the writer gave up that particular kind of 'good work' after three months' service on the train; three very happy months where such minor personal discomforts as difficulties with one's laundry, and even sometimes with one's personal cleanliness, were all lost sight of in the feeling that one was doing real work.

Work on an Ambulance Train in France, 1917-18
by Sister J. Orchardson, QAIMNS written during the later years of the war, when things had become a little more sophisticated.

I joined an Ambulance train at Rouen in December, 1917, proceeding up the line to the Somme Valley. My first impressions were the extreme cleanliness, order, and brightness of everything on the train. The sisters' mess, planned out of an ordinary railway carriage, was cosy and pretty, and our bedrooms most comfortable. Each train carried three sisters, usually a happy and contented trio. Our life was never dull, for those railways were the highroads of the war. Wherever we went there were troop trains, ammunition trains, food supplies, guns, tank stores; the never-ending accompaniments of a great campaign. Seldom were two days alike, no one knew where we might be sent next, or what adventure awaited us on the road. Our train might be in garage somewhere up the line, awaiting orders. All day nothing would happen and we would retire to bed at the usual hour. Suddenly there would be a bump, the signal that our engine had come on, and away we would go into the night wondering as to our destination. Wonder, however, soon gave place to sleep and we were content to leave place of call for the morning to disclose.

On loading at a Casualty Clearing Station, I was always struck by the rapidity and ease with which the patients were taken on and put to bed. I marvelled at their unfailing good humour, even when seriously wounded. They seemed to be so delighted to be on their way to the base, or perhaps to England, that they never failed to don a brave disguise. Somehow, I always felt more sorry for the walking wounded – that slow procession of pain with their white tired faces – but never a grumble or complaint. When loading was finished, our immediate duties were to inspect all the medical cards, diet the patients, and take a note of all treatments to be given during the journey; after this had been carried out, cigarettes, sweets, and books were handed round, and the sisters usually had time for a chat with the patients. On reaching the base the train was quickly unloaded, beds changed and made up again, wards scrubbed out and everything made ready for the next journey. The train usually remained for a few hours to take on stores, which gave us the opportunity to go shopping for our mess. Then up the line again, or best of all load up with patients for England. The latter was a joyous thing. We would take them to Calais or Le Havre and see them safely aboard the ship that was bound for 'Blighty'. Our train life was often very exciting, air raids were frequent and not seldom we had narrow escapes, when the windows of the coaches were shattered with the concussion of the explosives. Upon running into an air raid, all lights which were always well shaded, were put out and the train brought to a standstill. We could not help tremendously admiring the splendid bravery of the poor wounded men. They never once appeared afraid or complained, all they wanted was a cigarette. Their wonderful spirit gave us the courage to carry on. Had it not been for their dauntless spirit I feel certain that we should often have given in. Although badly wounded, they never seemed to turn a hair amid the most awful bombing and shelling. It was truly magnificent.

Our train was in the Somme Retreat of 1918, when the roads were crowded with retreating French civilians, leading their horses and cattle, and taking away what household goods they could carry. Old men and women, young women and children made a pathetic spectacle in that picture of retreat. The retreat began on March 23rd, 1918, and on the 25th the train was sent to Edgehill – a few miles from Albert – to load. We took the last patients from the Casualty Clearing Station at Edgehill and many straight from the field. The train was loaded to its full capacity; stretchers were put on the floors, in the corridors, in the two kitchens, and in the medical officers' and orderlies' beds. The train was held up for thirty-six hours but eventually reached Rouen. In April, the train was up north when the German offensive began and on several occasions took down a number of French civilians. One incident was most pathetic. When the enemy broke through at Merville there was the usual retreat of French people. The train was stopped by some soldiers who asked us to take an old French woman whom they had found lying on the roadside. She must have walked many miles and was in a pitiful state. She said she was eighty-two years of age, and we recalled the old Hebrew's saying about the years that only bring labour and sorrow. In June the train was sent to the Marne to assist the French, and took several loads of French wounded, with a few British, from the French advanced hospitals. The poilu is a most grateful patient and so appreciative of the smallest thing done for him. When they came on to the train and were given English cigarettes their delight was great. I asked a few if they would like to write home, and soon was busy supplying pencils and paper, so keen were these men to write to their people. Late June found the train at Charmes, near Nancy, and as this was the first khaki train to do this trip, we had a wonderful reception the whole of the way. Everywhere the French people were most enthusiastic. On the return journey the train stopped at a junction for an hour or more, and several French ladies asked permission to visit the patients. They brought baskets of fruit and sweets for the patients and presented the sisters with a bouquet of crimson roses, tied with the colours of fair and gallant France. Although at times a strenuous life, it was always a bright and happy experience, with just a touch of sadness when 'good-bye' was said at the journey's end. Looking back on those unforgettable days, I shall always see their faces, even as the faces that look out of some old and treasured picture book.

From September 1917 until June 1918 Staff Nurse Susan 'Susie' Greaves of the Queen Alexandra's Imperial Military Nursing Service Reserve worked on No 22 Ambulance Train on the Western Front and in Italy

The Newcastle Sun reported that 'Sister Greaves found the train life most interesting. It made her realise ... the devastation being almost beyond comprehension, especially on the Somme, where the train passed through miles and miles of ruin – only shell-holes and graves to mark where towns had once stood. What had once been a city was marked only by a pile of ruins ... While in Northern France, early in 1918, it was impossible to get a night's rest owing to the continuous air raids'.

Barry Hancock

Acknowledgements
I am most grateful to Alison Kay at the National Railway Museum for help and use of material from her NRM lecture and Sue Light of ScarletFinders (a web site dedicated to nurses who served in the Great War) who has helped me chase up the only Sheffield story I can find and allowed me to copy first hand accounts from the QA nurse memoirs that she has collected. The Liddle Collection (Leeds University) was the source of many original documents, particularly with regard to the Friends Ambulance Unit. Websites that I have accessed, and used material from, include National Library of Scotland, QARANC, Picture Postcards from the Great War, RAMC in the Great War, the Western Front Association, Great War Nurses from the Hunter, National Railway Museum and Imperial War Museum.

Sheffield's Military Hospitals in the Great War

Wartime British deaths came to number about three-quarters of a million, and almost two million others required medical attention. More than two and a half million soldiers were returned to this country for hospital treatment, of which around half were formally defined as 'sick' rather than 'wounded'. Although press reports and everyday conversations referred (and still refer) to 'wounded soldiers' or 'casualties' in the city and elsewhere, implying that they had been damaged by the enemy, many patients (although ill because of war service) had not themselves been injured by German weapons.

Immediately in August 1914 the War Office mobilized the territorial forces of its Royal Army Medical Corps. Plans had been prepared, and very soon twenty-three (later twenty-five) general military hospitals were opened around the country. One of these 'territorial hospitals' was in Sheffield – the Third Northern General Hospital. In addition to a central 'base', this came to include more than fifty associated units in the city and nearby. A second new category of provision was from already-established facilities which became converted and designated as 'war hospitals'. Ultimately numbering about eighty, these were set up in asylums and similar buildings administered by county councils and other public bodies after current inmates had been transferred elsewhere. Locally in this category, the Wadsley Asylum became the Wharncliffe War Hospital.

In a very short period of time, these two Sheffield hospitals were able to provide more than 6,000 beds for military patients. Although many of these were seriously ill, requiring intensive and possibly long-term treatment, a large number had reached the convalescent stage. These were placed in convalescent units and might be allowed to spend time outside their hospital. Invalid soldiers thus became a common sight around Sheffield, wearing a 'going-out' uniform of light-blue cloth with white lapels. Across all years of the war, Sheffield's military hospitals received in excess of 70,000 men.

The Third Northern General Hospital

This had been established by the Royal Army Medical Corps as a territorial unit in 1913. Soon after war was declared, the Corps requisitioned the Teachers' Training College located in Ecclesall Road and Collegiate Crescent. The College's three principal and other buildings were refurbished and equipped with operating theatres, an X-ray unit and other facilities, and on 3rd September 1914 the first patients arrived from the Western Front.

3rd Northern General Hospital, Ecclesall Road, Sheffield
©Sheffield Libraries and Archives

Initial medical staff came mainly from hospitals in the city, with Mr (now Lieutenant-Colonel) Arthur Connell as Commanding Officer. He was an honorary surgeon at the Royal Infirmary with consulting rooms in Glossop Road. Also from the Royal Infirmary, Dr A. G. Yates was appointed as Registrar with the rank of Major, and staff drawn from the Royal Hospital included Drs (now Lieutenant-Colonels) J. Sinclair White and W. S. Porter. Among the Hospital's clinical staff were eight professors or lecturers from Sheffield University, and the Ecclesall Road 'base' came to employ around twenty-five doctors and more than two hundred nurses; Matrons were drawn at different times from the Royal Hospital or Royal Infirmary. About sixty volunteer nurses (VADs) also worked in the 'base', and two local clergymen served as visiting Chaplains in addition to a resident army Chaplain. RAMC staff numbered around two hundred, and, several dozen support workers were employed for cooking, cleaning, maintenance and similar jobs.

As the number of patients increased during 1915 and 1916, the base in Ecclesall Road expanded within its large grounds. (Huts containing additional wards and recreation facilities were partly financed by voluntary contributions.) More serious cases were treated in the Ecclesall Road base, the Royal Hospital and the Royal Infirmary, and other patients were housed in new auxiliary and convalescent units elsewhere. Overall in the Hospital around 4,600 beds had become available by 1918, including some 2,600 in the city:

Ecclesall Road Base, 438 beds
Royal Infirmary, 87 beds
Royal Hospital, 80 beds
Winter Street Hospital, 134 beds
Firvale Hospital, 462 beds
Carterknowle School, 115 beds
Lydgate Lane School, 130 beds
Ranmoor School, 110 beds

Greystones School, 150 beds
Shiregreen School, 145 beds
Firshill School, 150 beds
Western Road School, 70 beds
Ecclesall Infirmary, 200 beds
Endcliffe Hall, 130 beds
Oakbrook Officers' Hospital, 51 beds
Bramall Lane Cricket Pavilion, 150 beds

Around thirty affiliated institutions provided some 2,000 beds for less serious cases. Within Sheffield were St John's Hospital at Dore and the Woofindin Convalescent

Home in Whiteley Wood, and outside the city were (for example) Longshaw Lodge at Grindleford, Aston Hall in Derby, Loversall Hall in Doncaster, and the Devonshire Hospital in Buxton.

The Royal Hospital allocated its Fulwood Road Annexe and three wards in its main building to military patients, and the Royal Infirmary offered a hundred of its 350 beds. For three years both these voluntary hospitals (in this period general hospitals received their income from charitable 'voluntary' donations from the public) treated military patients without charge to the government, but financial problems became steadily worse and from September 1917 they both accepted from the War Office the usual payment of four shillings (£0.20) a day for each soldier they treated.

During 1915, seven of the city's schools became hospitals. For example, in October, Carterknowle School was converted for patients from the Western Front and the Dardanelles, with a nursing sister, three nurses and two VAD nurse helpers; volunteer assistants undertook cooking and other tasks. Items such as a piano, gramophone and billiard table were all donated, as were chairs, kitchen equipment and hot water bottles. Lydgate School in Crosspool also opened as a hospital in October 1915 – with a sister-in-charge, five nurses, two VAD helpers and many volunteers. The large majority of the first year's patients in Lydgate Hospital suffered from dysentery and other intestinal complaints, with a smaller number being treated for gun-shot or shrapnel wounds, shell-shock and other results of enemy action. Unfortunately, patient records for this and other Sheffield hospitals are no longer available, so it is not possible to determine the overall mix of problems treated in the city. It is likely that different parts of the Third Northern General Hospital focused on different kinds of disorder, but details are lacking.

Firvale and Ecclesall Hospitals were located in the city's two Workhouse infirmaries; overall, Firvale treated as many as 10,000 wounded and sick soldiers and carried out around 1,000 operations. Endcliffe Hall in Ranmoor was converted to provide eight military wards, including one of thirty-two beds in the Hall's ball-room. Its large glass conservatory was used as an open-air ward after the roof had been removed. Next door to Endcliffe Hall was (and is) Oakbrook, which in the spring of 1917 became a hospital for around fifty officers. It had been offered rent-free to the War Office, and furniture and equipment were funded through a special appeal by the Lord Mayor to local firms and individual businessmen.

Many convalescent units of the Third Northern Hospital were outside Sheffield, but one was located in Dore. This was St John's Hospital, improvised in October 1914 in the Church Institute on Abbbeydale Road South and at first staffed entirely by volunteers: Red Cross nurses, cooks, cleaners and other helpers. Furniture, food and money were provided by local people both at the outset and through subsequent fund-raising events. St John's Hospital subsequently became a convalescent unit within the Third Northern General Hospital and cared also for British and Empire troops. In at least the early days, a local general practitioner doctor visited regularly and was on call as needed.

Just outside the city was Longshaw Lodge convalescent hospital. This was made available in early 1915 by the Duke of Rutland (it was his shooting lodge) and came to accommodate around sixty men, including many (referred to as 'colonials') from Dominions of the Empire. In addition to a small number of RAMC soldiers, staff included two nursing sisters within the Third Northern General Hospital and three VAD nursing assistants, supported by a laundress and other workers. As was usual, the government paid a fee for each patient, but running costs were greater than the allowance available and (as in other cases) Sheffield's Lord Mayor appealed for donations from the public; many gifts of money, food and other items were received from individuals and groups throughout the war.

Wharncliffe War Hospital

Most military hospitals of the second type described at the beginning of the chapter had previously been an asylum for mental patients. At Wadsley, some three miles from Sheffield's centre was the South Yorkshire Asylum, and this was taken over by the Royal Army Medical Corps at the beginning of April 1915. Inmates were transferred to other institutions or sent home, and the Asylum was renamed as Wharncliffe War Hospital. Up to its closure in August 1920, the Hospital treated almost 40,000 serving and discharged soldiers.

The new War Hospital had around 1,750 beds, although for a period in 1917 it was forced to accommodate more than 2,000 patients. It was staffed primarily by the Royal Army Medical Corps, and was newly fitted with its own X-ray machine and three operating theatres. The Commanding Officer, Lieutenant-Colonel William Vincent (previously and subsequently Director of the Asylum), and the Registrar, Major D. Gillespie, were assisted by a total of around twenty-five resident or visiting doctors. The Hospital's matron, sisters and nurses were accommodated in their own buildings on the site, and some of the previous Asylum staff were appointed as assistants. Five chaplains were available for patients of Church of England, Nonconformist and Roman Catholic religions.

Other Local Units

The overwhelming majority of military patients in Sheffield were treated in the newly-created hospitals described above, but a few were instead placed in the existing sixty-five-bed hospital within Hillsborough Barracks. Another medical unit making a significant military contribution was the charity-based Edgar Allen Institute. Each year this provided out-patient physiotherapy treatment (founded on the Swedish system of physical exercises) for around 1,000 soldiers from the city's military hospitals in addition to its civilian patients.

The city's fledgling University also served the war effort. Relevant to this chapter was the establishment in November 1915 of a volunteer-operated Hospital Supply Depot. Co-ordinated by wives of medical and other academics, some 500 women worked at different times (with a daily average of seventy-five) to prepare bandages, medical dressings, operation sheets and other items for dispatch to military hospitals. The Depot was registered as a charity, and money to purchase material and to fund the delivery of finished items came through flag days, concerts and donations from hundreds of local people; as was usual in the period, all donors and their contributions were listed in the city's newspapers. In the summer of 1916, the Depot established a section to prepare and dispatch surgical dressing pads made of sphagnum moss collected from moorland in the neighbourhood and elsewhere. Across all its work the Depot supplied nearly half a million articles to more than ninety hospitals in the United Kingdom and abroad, with most being sent locally.

Part of the University's Hospital Supply Depot was a separately-housed Surgical Supply Branch operating in conjunction with Civil Engineering staff. Around forty-five volunteers (including several of the city's school-teachers) worked throughout the war, often including evenings and weekends, to design and manufacture hundreds of wooden and metal surgical aids, instruments and appliances and items of hospital furniture. Some of the surgical items were tailor-made for individual patients in the city, requiring special measurement and personal fitting, and overall the Surgical Branch supplied equipment to more than forty military hospitals in the city and elsewhere.

Peter Warr

More details of these hospitals and events in the city are available in Peter Warr's *'Sheffield in the Great War'*, published by Pen and Sword Books in August 2014.

University activities are described in *'Sheffield's Great War and Beyond'* by Peter Warr, published by Pen and Sword Books in April 2015.

Professor Arthur Mayers Connell

My Grandfather was born in St Philip, Barbados on the 2nd March 1872 the third child of Joseph and Ellen Connell. The Connell family are believed to have migrated to Barbados in the 1670s from England, and pursued a life in the sugar industry. He was educated at the Lodge School with an open scholarship and, as a young man, met Emily Mary Sealy, the daughter of Dr. John Sealy, a near neighbour. His association with Dr. Sealy's daughter decided him that he wanted to pursue a career in medicine. Having finished his education in Barbados in 1890, he left for London.

He had the good fortune to enter University College at one of the peak times in its history. Heath, Victor Horsley and Raymond Jackson were the teachers who moulded the skills that he attained for his life as an eminent surgeon. His first contact with the Sheffield Royal Infirmary was as a resident student during a holiday in 1895, the year that he qualified. His experience at the Royal Infirmary made him determined to return. His first appointment following qualification was at the Fever Hospital in Birmingham, but in 1896 he got his wish and was appointed as a Junior House Surgeon at the Sheffield Royal Infirmary – the start of an amazing career that lasted almost 50 years. In 1899 he obtained the FRCS Ed. and was elected an Honorary Surgeon to the Sheffield Royal Infirmary on the 1st May. My Grandfather came to Sheffield at a critical period in the development of the Medical School. There was little surgery done beyond what was necessary for dealing with accidents, ruptures and suppuration. There was no University. He would describe the difficulties in those early days. There were no lifts, a theatre at the top of the building, lit by moveable inverted gas-jets served by a long rubber tube, from bracket to wall-pipe on which someone always trod when more illumination was required. A wooden operating table, carbolic acid spray and little preparation of patients skin, instruments, or surgeons hands. In conjunction with the late Archibald Cuff, my Grandfather introduced

Lt Col Arthur Mayers Connell

modern surgical ideas and techniques into the Royal Infirmary and, with Sir Arthur Hall, played no small part in the foundation of the University.

Some time in late 1901 or early 1902 Emily Mary Sealy arrived in England and on the 17th September 1902 she and my Grandfather were married at the Parish Church of St Mary Magdaline, Hastings, in Sussex. It seemed an odd location to get married since my Grandfather was already living and had a permanent position at the Infirmary in Sheffield. However, they returned to Sheffield and set up house in Taptonville Crescent in a large 4/5 bedroom house where all his children Ellen, John and Arthur were born. Sadly, on the 26th June 1917, my Grandmother, Emily, known as Milly, died following a short illness leaving three young children, the youngest being only five.

In 1900, Grandfather became Assistant Demonstrator in Anatomy and Pathology at the Medical School and it was the department which held his interest for the rest of his life. He became Lecturer in Operative Surgery in 1904, lecturer in Surgery in 1911 and Professor in 1919. In common with other members of his family in Barbados, Grandfather was a keen Territorial soldier. He first joined in London in 1891 the Volunteer Medical Staff Corps but in 1902 he joined the 4th West Yorkshire Volunteer Artillery so it was no wonder that at the outbreak of the Great War he would become involved with the Royal Army Medical Corps.

The extensive buildings that originally formed the Collegiate School in Collegiate Crescent, later became the Royal Grammar School in the 1880s. In 1906 they were converted to the Sheffield Training College for Teachers. In 1914 the buildings were requisitioned and became the 3rd Northern General (Base) Hospital, and my Grandfather was put in command with the rank of Lieut. Colonel RAMC. In 1917 he was promoted to Brevet Colonel and became a Consultant Surgeon to Northern Command. He was appointed Assistant Director of Medical Services (ADMS) of a division of the Eastern Counties. In 1919 he became district Consultant Surgeon to the southern portion of Northern Command. During the Great War frequent visits were made by my Grandfather together with fellow officers and nurses to field hospitals in both France and Belgium. Many badly wounded soldiers were transferred to the 3rd Northern General for treatment. At the end of the war Grandfather met the King of The Belgians who made him an Officer in the Order of Leopold. Many tributes have been made about my Grandfather's work at the 3rd Northern General (Base) Hospital but it can be summed up by a letter to the Editor of the Sheffield Telegraph in 1931 as follows: *'The thing that will stand out most prominently in his life will be his great work at the Base Hospital. We may not all, agree on the war, but we can at least agree that those who by their skill and loving care helped to alleviate the suffering caused by the war, deserve our sincere thanks. I am sure there are hundreds who will share this opinion'.* At the end of the war my Grandfather married again. On the 19th June 1919 he married Annie Roper, known as Nance, and they lived at Taptonville Crescent, later moving to Endcliffe Rise Road. Nance died on the 27th June 1944.

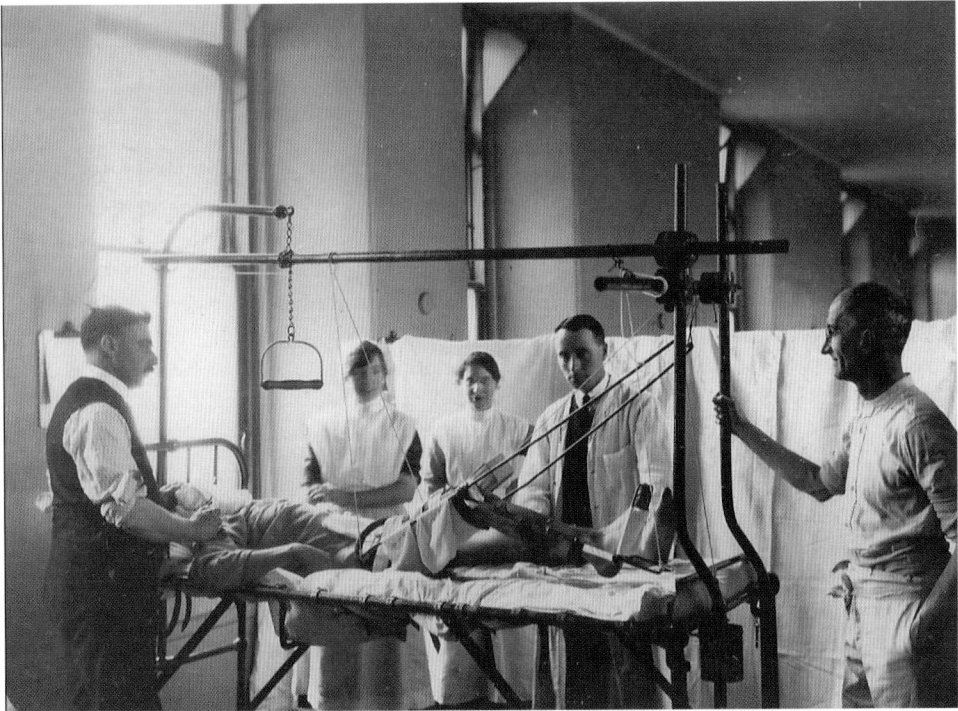

A surgical ward in the Royal Infirmary, Sheffield in 1921.
From L. to R. Mr. Norton Milner, Dr. Inman - House Surgeon, Professor A. M. Connell

In addition to his work at the Royal Infirmary, and a lecturer at the University, he was appointed Deputy Coroner to the City of Sheffield, a position he held from 1924 to 1937. He continued his work at the Royal Infirmary and his teaching of surgery and pathology at the Medical School until his retirement. This was accepted by the Board of the Infirmary, with great regret. He had been associated with the Royal Infirmary for 35 years and the University for 31 years. Many individuals in the City of Sheffield considered that his work be acknowledged. The Lord Mayor decided to inaugurate a fund to raise £1000 to endow a bed at the Royal Infirmary in recognition of his work. Finally the sum of £652 / 8s / 5p was collected. An illuminated book was presented to him in February 1933 with the names of the Endowment Fund Committee together with all the names of those who subscribed to the Fund. A tablet was unveiled above the Connell Bed in No 6 Ward and was dedicated by the Bishop of Sheffield who said: *'his mind went back to the time when Col. Connell attended wounded soldiers, who spoke of his skill, unending patience, and power of holding affection of those who were strangers to him'*. In addition to the endowment of a bed in his name, it was decided by the Weekly Board and the Honorary Medical Staff of the Infirmary to present him with his portrait which was painted by Mr. H. G. Hoyland RBA. This portrait still hangs in the Royal Hallamshire Hospital in Sheffield. A copy is in my possession to be handed down to the future generations as evidence of his great skill and devotion. Although my Grandfather had retired from the Infirmary and the University he continued to be involved in other hospitals in the Sheffield area. He was visiting Consultant Surgeon to the Montagu Hospital, Mexborough and the Fullerton Hospital, Denaby Main where he treated many miners who thought highly of his work in dealing with the many grave fracture cases which colliery work create.

During the Second World War his elder son Dr. John Connell was medical officer at No 16 Balloon centre at RAF Norton. On many occasions my Father was privileged to have his Father assist him in the theatre. This was recognised in 1941 by Air Marshall Gossage, Commanding Officer Balloon Command expressing their sincere gratitude, but also that of the Air Ministry, for the many occasions he had given his surgical assistance. He continued working during the war with his association to the Montagu and Fullerton Hospitals together with helping his elder son at RAF Norton, but in November 1945 he suffered a heart attack and died on the 8th November, 1945.

In 1983, Mrs Ursula Clarke (the widow of Mr. John Gray, Consultant Ear, Nose and Throat Surgeon at the Royal Hospital, Sheffield.) made a presentation of a skull to the Pathology Museum at the University. Following the death of her first husband Mrs. Clarke married Dr. J. R. Clarke, a lecturer in Physics at the University. During the Great War, Captain Clarke who was in the King's Own Yorkshire Light Infantry was severely wounded leading his men over the top in France in 1915. He was deemed to be dead. His Batman went to the mortuary to collect his belongings but noticed the Captain was actually breathing. In spite of the great distance Captain Clarke was repatriated and admitted to the 3rd Northern General Hospital and placed in the care of my Grandfather. Captain Clarke had sustained a large shrapnel wound in his head. The only solution my Grandfather considered was to cover the gaping wound with a metal plate. Having measured the area he dispatched an Orderly to go to Mappin and Webb and ask that a gold plate be made according to the template. The said plate was then sewn in place by Grandfather covering the hole and it successfully healed.

In conclusion, I cannot do any better than quote from an Article that was written for the South Yorkshire Times and Express on the 17th November 1945:
'Arthur Connell, scientist, surgeon, soldier, and 'varsity don, has gone from us, leaving a vivid memory of a vital personality…
He was supreme and superb in his craft–his long, thin sensitive hands told you something about that – but he was also intensely human, tempted in all points like as we are, very much a man and a brother, and we miss and mourn him mainly on that account'.
For my own part, the more I read and research my Grandfather, I truly believe he was the most remarkable person – highly gifted as a teacher and surgeon, well before his time, with strong Christian beliefs and generous to a fault.

Miles S. Connell.

'We are frightfully proud of her' – Sheffield Nurses and the First World War

The First World War was unlike previous wars. It was fought not only on foreign fields by a professional army; it involved the whole population of men, women and children across Europe, Africa and half the world's oceans. Machine guns, motor traction and aeroplanes caused unprecedented rates of disease, injury and death. Trench warfare exposed combatants to lice infestations, typhoid and dysentery. Terrible wounds were inflicted and contamination led to sepsis and gas gangrene. Chemicals developed for industrial use during the nineteenth century were deployed as weapons. Psychological trauma was common.

At the outbreak of War, nursing, teaching, dressmaking, and domestic service were deemed suitable jobs for women, although most married women never expected to work outside the home. With war, demand for uniforms, steel for tanks and aircraft and ammunition grew. Women, and men unfit to fight, filled vacancies in Sheffield's steelworks and munitions factories left by soldiers – female trade union membership rose from 350 to 5,000 between 1914 and 1918. Contemporary British societal understanding was that caring and nurturing were extensions of women's domestic roles, making nursing an obvious outlet for their talents. Women volunteered to work in hospitals and convalescent homes. By Armistice in 1918, 1,000,000 had served as nurses and all women who had worked in some capacity in wartime hospitals were described as 'nurses', whether trained professionals or not. During the War, Sheffield hospitals treated people who worked in the munitions factories, civilians injured by bombing, and met the normal requirements of a large urban population. Surgery allowed Sheffield men, prevented from enlisting because of 'surgical defects', to go to war. In September 1914, a month after war broke out, the first convoys of sick and wounded soldiers arrived from the Front. By 1916, approximately 20,000 military patients had been brought to the city, and they continued to arrive until 1920. This article aims to explore nursing in Sheffield on the Home Front during the War.

It was only after Florence Nightingale went to the Crimea in 1854 that a modern nursing service was established in the British Army and this was followed by the formation of an army nursing service in 1881. By 1914 the small but well-established Queen Alexandra Imperial Military Nursing Service (QAIMNS), provided nurses for military hospitals in the United Kingdom and overseas. It had a naval counterpart, and each was supported by reservists. From 1909, the Territorial Force Nursing Service (TFNS) provided thousands of volunteer, trained civilian nurses ready to nurse on the Home Front. In addition, the First Aid Nursing Yeomanry (FANY) was founded in 1907, formed of women trained in cavalry work, signalling and camping out who could drive ambulances and bring first aid to casualties in the field. Nevertheless, nursing numbers were inadequate to meet the demand for skilled care and the Government turned to volunteers for help. County branches of the British Red Cross and the St John's Ambulance Brigade organised Voluntary Aid Detachments (VADs) in which over 70,000 volunteered, two thirds of them female. Vera Brittain described volunteers as *'usually upper-middle class women who could afford to work and travel without pay'*. Unaccustomed to traditional hospital discipline and lacking advanced skills, their presence was often resented by professional nurses who feared it was undermining the fight for Nurse Registration. War had interrupted both this and the campaign for female suffrage. Yet supported by trained nurses to gain clinical experience, VADs were soon seen as indispensable.

The first Florence Nightingale Training School for nurses was founded at London's St Thomas' Hospital in 1860 and a prescribed training period soon established nursing as a respectable middle-class women's profession. A nurse training school was started at the Sheffield Royal Infirmary in 1898 and the Royal Hospital and the Union Hospital at Fir Vale also offered nurse training. Trained civilian nurses might also belong to the city's Territorial Force Nursing Service (TFNS) unit who worked at the Third Northern General Hospital Base Hospital from 1914. Female nurses in the QAIMNS and its Reserves and their male counterparts in the Royal Army Medical Corps and reserves also worked at Wharncliffe War Hospital. VADs worked in the Base and War Hospitals, as well as VAD hospitals – such as St John's, Abbeydale, Dore.

Wounded servicemen from the Front arrived in Britain aboard a hospital ship and were then taken by convoy to one of a nationwide network of Base Hospitals. These administrative units grouped buildings ranging from schools to cricket pavilions, turning them into hospitals. Beds were offered to the military authorities by the Royal Infirmary, Royal Hospital and Fir Vale Hospital. Civilian patients continued to be accommodated in wards sometimes occupied by soldiers. Beds were also provided in the city's fever hospitals. The men's Teacher Training College in Ecclesall Road became the headquarters of the Third Northern General Base Hospital, which incorporated several school buildings, a cricket pavilion and a large country house at Longshaw in Derbyshire. VAD hospitals were also opened and VAD nurses gained ward nursing experience in Sheffield's Royal Hospital and Royal Infirmary, where the Matron suggested in 1918 that two years' VAD experience should equate to a year of hospital nursing training.

Both the Infirmary and the Hospital had completed expensive building projects during the early twentieth century funded by large bank overdrafts. One of the Hospital's Governors tried to persuade colleagues to apply for fees from the War Office to pay for the care of military sick and wounded. Between August 1914 and August 1917, 1474 wounded soldiers were nursed in the Hospital, their care costing a total of £8923. From June 1916 to December 1917 alone, the Hospital's expenditure exceeded income by over £2,700. It was only in 1917 that, having agreed to launch a joint public appeal for financial help, the Secretaries of both Boards wrote to ask Northern Command in York to start paying them fees to finance use of occupied beds. Later, both hospitals negotiated a small retainer for unoccupied beds on condition they be made immediately available for military use. Disagreement subsequently arose at the Hospital over responsibility for providing the nursing staff to care for military patients. The military authorities claimed the fees they paid should cover nursing costs but the Hospital could not provide the nurses, money notwithstanding. For several weeks military patients were temporarily removed before the military authorities agreed to supply the nursing staff and arrange their own laundering.

Wharncliffe War Hospital faced different challenges. Its staff was initially depleted as individuals enlisted, but by November 1914 the asylum was able to resume full 'off duty' arrangements. As a public asylum, funding was secure although meagre. The transformation of the asylum into a fully functioning general hospital, complete with operating theatres and X-ray department in a few weeks, was remarkable. Bar a few staying behind on the hospital farm, 1,700 patients were transferred around the West Riding of Yorkshire and beyond. All were photographed before transfer, and their names confirmed, whether or not the patients could or would cooperate. Many patients died after transfer, despite the endeavours of the asylum authorities. Wharncliffe War Hospital, as it became, was led by a cadre of QAIMNS nurses brought in by the War Office. The Asylum's female nurses became general probationers under the charge of the new senior nurses; the male attendants were drafted into the RAMC reserve. Sheffield Royal Infirmary's Matron agreed to provide two weeks' training for members of the Asylum's nursing staff in April 1915. Within the year, the nursing staff was supplemented by groups of soldiers sent from Hillsborough Barracks for two weeks at a time to learn the rudiments of ward nursing, with lectures in basic first aid and anatomy and physiology to prepare them to give battlefield first aid. The hospital reported that it was acting as a 'Training School' by the end of 1915.

Most nurses will have continued to work in Sheffield during the War. Others served at the Front with one of the military nursing services or, once its remit included service overseas, the TFNS. The matron of Sheffield Royal Hospital, and the Third Northern General Hospital, Miss Earle, TFNS, was decorated for service with the British Hospital in Basra, Mesopotamia.

At least two Sheffield-trained nurses received the Military Medal for bravery. Sister Mabel Louise Evans was nursing on Ambulance Train Number 27 when it was bombed. *'The Commanding Officer reports that this Sister, carrying a hand lamp, went about her work coolly and collectedly and cheerfully and that by her magnificent conduct she not only allayed alarm among the helpless patients and those suffering from shell shock but caused both patients and personnel to play up to the standards which she set'. (The London Gazette, 22 January 1917).*

The Commandant of Boulogne Casualty Clearing Station, wrote to Mary Agatha Brown's brothers:

Miss Earle, Matron of the 3rd Northern General Hospital. ©*Sheffield Libraries and Archives*

'Please accept the heartiest congratulations from all members of this CCS on your sister, Miss M. A. Brown, winning the Military Medal for conspicuous bravery. On March 21st a hostile bomb fell within a few yards of her, fatally wounding one sister and mortally wounding the matron. Miss Brown gallantly attended to them under fire of machine guns and bombs until help came, and later on worked hard for hours in the operating theatre. We are frightfully proud of her'.

Other Sheffield nurses received the Royal Red Cross decoration for their work. Nurses came to Sheffield from New Zealand, Australia and the United States but hospitals were hard-pressed to recruit sufficient nurses. The Infirmary increased probationer nurses' wages in 1917 and 1918, and they and other hospital authorities raised trained nurses' salaries to improve staff retention. Married nurses at Wharncliffe War Hospital were permitted to remain in post from mid-1917, although against regulations. Difficulty in securing suitable medical staff led the Infirmary to elect a woman to the medical staff in 1915 and in April 1917, Lieutenant Colonel Sinclair White proposed that:

'...owing to the shortage of resident officers, the Sisters of the surgical wards should be trained to give anaesthetics. This was agreed upon. The Matron was interviewed and saw no difficulty in this being carried out. The surgeon of the case to be responsible for any mishap.'

Wherever they worked, nurses whose experience had involved civilian nursing– even where this included industrial injuries sustained in the steelworks – learned to nurse men with bullet and shrapnel wounds, gas poisoning and mental disability – later termed shell-shock. Wharncliffe War Hospital received five convoys over four days in October 1915: *'I feel sure the Committee will realise what it means to receive 400 sick and terribly wounded men in four days. The cases have been exceedingly bad and the operating rooms and X ray Department has been kept well occupied indeed'.* By November 1915, the hospital had received 440 wounded and sick military patients in 26 convoys. Until 1920, the death rate among the military wounded and sick remained between 0.5 and 0.64%. Without antibiotics and with little beyond skilled nursing, this was a remarkable achievement. Several wound dressing changes daily might be required for each patient but cotton and gauze were in short supply; sphagnum moss, known for its absorbency, was used as an alternative because of its 'availability, cheapness and suitability'. In July 1916, The Sheffield Telegraph published photographs of women preparing wound dressings in Sheffield University Hospital Supplies Depot using sphagnum moss, which grew abundantly on the moors bordering Sheffield. One source noted *'Sphagnum Moss was also used during the War in conjunction with Garlic, one of the best antiseptics. The Government bought up tons of the bulbs, which were sent out to the front; the raw juice expressed, diluted with water, was put on swabs of sterilised Sphagnum Moss and applied to wounds. Where this treatment was adopted there were no specific complications, and thousands of lives were thus saved'. (Mrs. M. Grieve, 1931, 'A modern herbal').*

Wharncliffe War Hospital was remarkable in applying the skills and experience of its own staff to provide a 'mental block' for men who had suffered mental disability as a consequence of their experiences at the Front. Towards the end of the War, Wharncliffe's administrators – alone among Sheffield's hospitals - agreed to accommodate and treat men whose injuries necessitated long term hospital care. For several years after the war, one block was set aside as a Ministry of Pensions hospital for men from the Sheffield area.

The 1914-18 War was called 'The Great War' but there is nothing great about a war where half the youth of the world died or were damaged physically, mentally, spiritually or socially. Yet the War had also opened opportunities for nurses some of which would contribute to the emergence of entirely new health occupations and they would travel and work with nurses from across the world. Within a year of the Armistice, Nursing Registration was on the statute book and although this excluded VADs from joining the profession simply by virtue of experience, their contribution was sought during the Second World War, twenty years later.

Judy Redman and Paula Hancock

Many sources have been used in this article and more details of these can be obtained on request to j.h.redman@shu.ac.uk

The Edgar Allen Institute and the rehabilitation of military personnel in World War One

William Edgar Allen (1837–1915) was a Sheffield industrialist prominent in the growing Sheffield steel industry from which he made his fortune. However he was also a philanthropist of considerable generosity amongst other things endowing a purpose-built library for the University of Sheffield. For the ordinary Sheffielder however, his philanthropy was perhaps more remembered for the establishment of the Edgar Allen Institute which served the city in various forms for 77 years from its opening in 1911 until its final closure in 1988.

Edgar Allen himself, had been treated abroad using the Swedish Zander method of massage and exercise. The Zander method, invented by the Swede, Dr. Gustav Zander, was a method of therapeutic exercise based on graduated muscular resistance induced by machinery. In 1910, he decided to establish such an institute in Sheffield, the first such in the U.K. He sent, at his own expense a Sheffield doctor, Dr. R. C. Abercrombie, to study the method for six months at various venues. He became the first medical director of the Sheffield Institute for Medico-Mechanical Treatment, as the institute was first known. Edgar Allen generously undertook to to finance the creation of the unit and the running costs for the first 3 years. His aim was to provide a facility to apply physical treatment to patients suffering *'disease, injuries or accident and unable otherwise to obtain it'*. It was intended to help *'working men and women, wage earners to regain health and the use of their limbs as quickly as possible and enable them to return sooner to their work after injuries, accidents and illnesses'*. The Institute was opened in 1911 changing its name in 1912 to the Edgar Allen Institute (Incorporated) and, although not intended for the rehabilitation of war injuries, represented a modern well equipped unit easily adaptable to receive those injured on the battlefield.

The war wounded

It is perhaps a measure of the man that, on the outbreak of war, Mr. Allen offered the facility without charge for the rehabilitation of wounded and injured soldiers agreeing soon afterwards to employ an additional masseuse at his own expense to allow more soldiers to be accepted for treatment. The offer was rejected by the War Office, as later reported in a Sheffield newspaper on October 15th 1916, because *'the Institute was not a military hospital and could not be entirely taken over as such by reason of a proviso in the endowment in respect of civilian patients'*. Despite this the Institute was soon receiving the war wounded after the immediate medical treatment with the aim of restoring as much function as possible. Many wounded soldiers and sailors passed through the Institute's hands (nearly 1,500 from all over the country by October 1916) with many returned to active service.

Some of the treatment they received is illustrated in the following images:

In the case (left) a soldier with upper limb paralysis is learning fine movements with the aid of a wheel and an assistant

The illustration below shows how repetitive gentle tapping by a machine to the back of the soldier on the left is used as an aid to improve and restore balance to soldiers with spinal damage

Keeping the Institute solvent

Although the facility was offered to the Military at no charge the Institute had to be funded somehow, especially after the initial 3 years funding had expired just before the outbreak of war. Some of these costs were met by the charges paid by private patients or those referred by members having bought the right to refer patients. In some instances Insurance Companies, who would have been supporting the wage earners whilst out of work, were induced to make some payments on the grounds that their insured members would be off their books sooner with the treatment. This still left a shortfall and the Edgar Allen Institute Minute Book reveals that a request was made to the Military that a payment of one guinea should be made for each soldier treated but this was rejected as excessive. The Board suggested 15 shillings instead but with no response sought a meeting with Col. Connell at the Sheffield Base Hospital. After he realised that the 15 shillings was for the duration of treatment he agreed this was reasonable and promised to recommend acceptance to the War Office. As far as one can tell from the Minute Book no response was ever received, apart from the Military authorities regretting that it could not sanction a grant to the Institute. Nevertheless, soldiers continued to pass through the Institute unimpeded. On one occasion Col. Connell agreed to approach the Lord Mayor for a discretionary award and 25 guineas were received from the Lord Mayor's fund. The treated soldiers themselves, in gratitude for what they had received, came to the rescue in 1916 by suggesting a 'Flag Day'. This was set for April 21st, 1917, and realised £1,600. Further 'Special War Effort Flag Days' were held in 1918 and 1919 though the Minute Book does not record the amount raised.

Soldiers and Sailors discharged from the armed services

It is inevitable that some wounded soldiers would not be regarded as fit to re-join their units. These people would be discharged from the armed forces re-joining the ranks of civilians. Their continuing physical needs are the subject of numerous discussions recorded in the Minute Book. In January 1917, it was recorded that disabled and discharged soldiers from Sheffield and District would be treated without charge on the production of a referral note from a medical practitioner and a letter of recommendation from a War Pensions Committee. Whilst it was hoped to extend this to all discharged men at some point it is clear that those not from Sheffield would have to be regarded as paying civilians. In October of the same year, a letter from the Sheffield Local War Pensions Committee asked that discharged combatants from all services be treated at a charge of 2/6d for the first visit and 1/6d for subsequent visits. The Executive Committee of the Edgar Allen Institute accepted this whilst pointing out that this was actually below the actual cost to the Institute and that they retained the right to renegotiate or terminate the arrangement. Thus the Edgar Allen Institute played an important part in rehabilitating soldiers after war injuries both when they were still serving and even after they may have been discharged from the Armed Forces.

Rodney Amos

Sir Ernest Finch

Major Finch at the 3rd Northern General Hospital ©Sheffield Libraries and Archives

Ernest Finch was born in 1884, the son of Frederick James Finch and was educated at Commercial Travellers Schools, Hatch End, Middlesex. He gained an entrance scholarship to Sheffield University which at that time was without charter and unable to grant medical degrees. He qualified in 1906 as MB, BS London with honours in pathology. He served as casualty officer, house surgeon and surgical registrar at Sheffield Royal Infirmary and in 1912 was elected honorary assistant surgeon.

Like many of his colleagues he joined the territorial army and at the outbreak of war he held the rank of Major in the 3rd West Riding Field Ambulance. He served in France and later at the 3rd Northern General Hospital, and after the war he rapidly became the leading surgeon in the Sheffield area. He was appointed Honorary Professor of Surgery in 1933 until retirement in 1944. He was a popular teacher and delivered the Bradshaw and Vicary Lectures of the Royal College of Surgeons and became the Hunterian Lecturer in 1957. He served as President of the Association of Surgeons, of the Surgical Section of the Royal Society of Medicine and of the Sheffield Medico-Chirurgical Society and also of many committees of the Sheffield Regional Hospital Board. He was knighted in 1951 and was Vice President of the Royal College of Surgeons in 1953 and 1954. Also he received an Honorary DSc from Sheffield University

Ernest Finch had an extraordinary ability to inspire confidence in patients and their relatives by his gentleness and consideration. He was a great friend of young surgeons all over the country, but especially in Sheffield, never forgetting a pupil and keeping in close touch with many of them. Ernest Finch devoted his life to surgery, to the Sheffield Medical School and to the Royal College of Surgeons and the rapid development of the Medical School and the establishment of the departments of orthopaedics, neurosurgery and chest surgery are largely due to his foresight and enthusiasm. He died in 1960 at the age of 76 years after a long illness being survived by his wife, Mary, and son. He is remembered not only as a great surgeon, but as a kind and generous man.

Derek Cullen

A Brief History
of Prosthetic Limbs

A prosthesis is an artificial extension that replaces a missing body part. Historically, of all machines, it has the closest proximity with the human body but the least chance of matching its performance. Since the first recordings of prosthetic limbs, development has changed very little up to the first half of the 20th century. Prosthetic limbs were made of basic materials such as wood and metal with leather attachments

Prosthetic toe discovered in Cairo

or appendage. The first evidence of a prosthetic limb was a discovery made in 2,000 in Cairo. The mummified remains of a noblewoman 3,000 years old was wearing a prosthetic toe made of wood and leather. Previous to this find, the oldest prosthetic limb discovery was the Capua leg. This prosthetic below knee limb was found in a tomb in Capua, Italy. The limb dates back to 300 years BC and was made of copper.

One of the earliest accounts from ancient history was during the 2nd Punic War, 218-210 BC. Roman general Marcus Sergius lost his hand in battle. A hand fashioned out of iron was fitted for the purpose of holding a shield and he returned to battle. 2,000 years on in the 'dark ages', heavy iron limbs were crafted by metal workers for the knights who lost limbs in battle. These limbs were non-functional and served to disguise an embarrassing deformity. Generally the metal workers who constructed the prosthetic limbs were the armourers who manufactured the armour and weapons for the knights. Therefore, prosthetics and armourers have a strong alliance and could equally share the distinction of the second oldest profession in the world.

Famously, as portrayed in many epic films, pirates have worn peg legs and hook hands. This is factually correct although not confined to pirates. Anybody who sailed the seven seas could succumb to limb loss. Limbs were fashioned out of anything that was made available from the ship. Some of the material used to make the leg included bone, dense woods such as oak, light woods such as pine or even cork. Unfortunately for the pirate, they did not carry a ships surgeon and amputation was performed by the ships cook who had the sharpest knife. Success was very low.

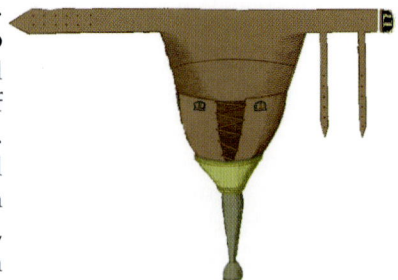

18th Century peg leg

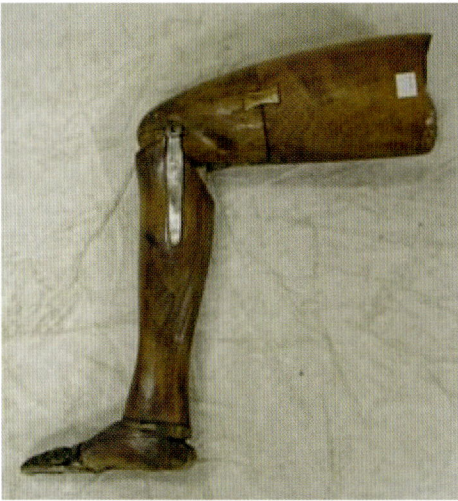

The locking knee – Pieter Verduyn

During the 16th century innovation was developing. French military doctor and barber surgeon Ambroise Paré invented mechanical hands and hinged knees. Such was his reputation; he became surgeon to 4 French Kings.

Dutch surgeon, Pieter Verduyn, developed locking knees and for the below knee amputee, a leather cuff strap suspension. Cuff straps and locking knees are still used today. In 1800, in London, James Potts designed a prosthetic leg made of wood. A steel knee joint was incorporated and an articulated foot that was controlled by 'cat gut' tendons from the knee to the ankle. Later on this limb became known as the Anglesey leg after the Marquis of Anglesey who lost his leg above the knee at the battle of Waterloo and wore the wooden limb.

In 1843, Sir James Symes revolutionised a method of ankle disarticulation which didn't need to amputate at the thigh or shank. The possibility of walking again with foot prosthesis versus leg prosthesis was a realistic possibility. The Symes disarticulation is a common site of amputation today and is extensively used with children. It encourages walking on a weight bearing surface without cut bone. The growth plate is maintained although a little slower on the Symes side. This allows space for more dynamic foot components.

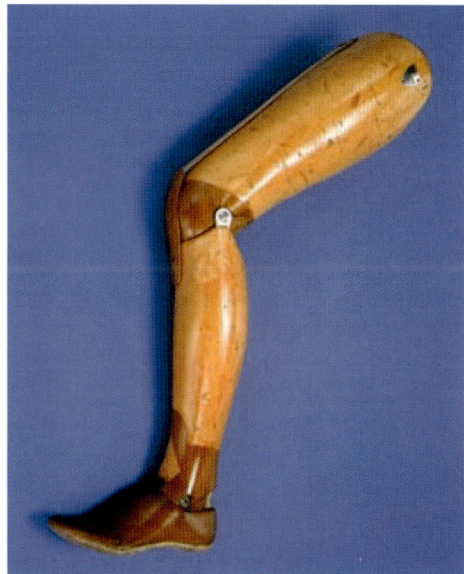

Anglesey leg

The American civil war began in 1861. The first conflict between Union and Confederate forces was at the battle of Philippi. James Edgar Hangar was a young trooper on the Confederate side. He was hit by cannon shot in the leg and became, probably, the first amputee of the war. After discharge from hospital, J. E. Hangar confined himself to his bedroom at his parents' home for many weeks. Meals and refreshments were placed outside his door. Eventually Hangar emerged from his room and walked silently down the stairs to the front room on a leg he had designed and built himself. The limb was later patented as the Hangar limb. It was so effective that the state commissioned him to manufacture limbs for other civil war veterans.

1868 Gustav Hermann suggested using Aluminium as a lighter material to replace steel. It wasn't until 1912 that an Englishman, Marcel Desoutter, was involved in an airplane accident and manufactured an aluminium limb for himself. The start of the 20th century had every reason to be innovative and pro-active. Unfortunately World War One did not provoke a prosthetic response immediately. Before the war, the profession of manufacture of artificial limbs was an industry known little to the UK. Soon the stimulus was ignited and provoked the invention, improvement and production of artificial limbs. Peg legs were still utilised extensively and a cheaper lightweight version was even introduced. Specialist centres were now established and the UK looked at America for inspiration. J. F. Rowley and J. E. Hangar had manufactured limbs similar to those in use in the UK. Based on the Anglesey or Hangar limb, the American limb was still wooden in construction. A new development was a single strap that passed over the shoulder and attached to the leg below the knee to act as a mechanism for extension. The 'cat gut' tendons were removed and replaced with Indian rubber buffers in the foot. The whole limb was covered in parchment or rawhide. It wasn't just the Americans who answered the call. Very reputable companies such as Chas. A. Blatchford in the UK also made a huge contribution to the rehabilitation of 240,000 amputees from the Great War. It was quite apparent that the Americans dominated the prosthetic industry in WW1. With thousands of amputees coming back from the trenches, the small back room limb makers had to move on to a bigger industry.

Lessons learnt from the Spanish Civil War were taken into account at the onset of WW2. The potential for aircraft to fly long range and bomb industrial cities was achievable. The civilian population was at high risk. The manufacture of prosthetic limbs was stepped up. The initial British yearly output was 5,000 per year. A stock pile of 25,000 artificial limbs was proposed to be manufactured each year. It was deemed necessary to store these limbs in case Roehampton succumbed to the blitz. The stock piled limbs were to be peg legs with no articulating joints. They were to be made of wood, specifically willow which was abundant in the UK. Metal limbs were manufactured throughout the war. They were made from aluminium but the quality was generally poor. The specification of the aluminium was downgraded to allow for the higher specification aluminiums to be used for the manufacture of material to be used for the war effort.

It wasn't until the early 1980s that lighter modular limbs were introduced as the mainstay of prosthetic manufacture. The sockets were manufactured from polypropylene and resins. The functional components such as knees and feet were made of higher grade steels and aluminiums. These components could be mixed and matched to provide optimum performance to the amputee.

Modern modular limbs   *Modular limb with cosmoses*

A more lifelike finish could be provided to produce a cosmetic finish. Socket manufacture, modular components and cosmesis has moved on a pace but with a cost. High strength and lightweight carbon fibres are used extensively. High impact components are titanium and high definition silicones provide a very realistic look. Limbs today can be provided for any activity an amputee wishes to pursue. They can be used in water or components fitted to enable high activities and sporting events. Micro-processors now provide realistic body function in real time. The use of strain gauges and pneumatics and hydraulics allow for a safe, smooth function.

Howard David

August 1914 – the Entrepreneur's worrisome day . . .

Tuesday, 4th August, 1914, should have been an auspicious day for Mr. John William Northend. After successfully setting up his thriving general printing business in Norfolk Row in 1889, he was in the throes of opening his new, purpose-built, printing office located at 49 West Street, Sheffield. By June 1914, the building was almost completed and J.W.N. knew he must make preparations for the removal of his presses and equipment. However, rumours of war were rife and he was getting worried: a European political crisis appeared to be coming to a head. The big question was, could the removal be completed before war broke out, when restrictions might be imposed?

By 1914, his four sons had reached their majority. Lewis Alfred aged 32, Edgar Thornton aged 28, and William Frederick aged 26 had been educated at the Sheffield Central Secondary School, whilst the youngest son Ernest aged 22, had been educated, as a boarder, at the Society of Friends School in Ackworth, near Pontefract. By 1914, each son was making progress in his chosen career. In 1896, the eldest son, Lewis joined the printing business but he had already made up his mind on an alternative career in journalism and after working for two or three years as a printer, he left with the blessing of his father, to become a junior reporter at the Sheffield Daily Independent. He rose, by stages, to become Chief Reporter and when in 1908, an evening paper was launched under the title of The Mail, he became its Editor. In 1910, he took up an editorial appointment on the Manchester Guardian but within two years, he was invited to transfer to the Guardian's Parliamentary reporting staff in Fleet Street. Within a year an even better offer came from The Times where he became the Parliamentary Correspondent and later, the Labour Affairs Correspondent.

With the departure of Lewis into journalism it seemed fitting that one of the other sons should join the firm. However, Edgar Thornton Northend, the second son, on leaving school, had become articled to a firm of electrical engineers. After some negotiation, his articles were broken, and the premium forfeited. By the time Edgar started work as a printer the firm was well-established. His father was a friend of the illustrious typographer, George W. Jones and both were in the van of the Arts and Crafts Movement. His father viewed closely the technical developments which were taking place in the German printing industry and he arranged for Edgar to widen his knowledge by spending two years in a printing house in Leipzig and, at the same time, acquire fluency in the German language.

Edgar returned to Germany again in July 1914, this time as guide and interpreter to a visiting party from the British Federation of Master Printers. The visit took place only a week before the outbreak of the war, the delegates were taken for a flight in a Zeppelin and finally they returned to England via the fast regular cross-channel route, leaving their luggage to be shipped by a freight transport steamer. The freighter bound for England was the first ship of the war to be sunk in the English Channel following the outbreak of hostilities.

William F. Northend

The third Northend son, William Frederick was, from an early age, earmarked to become the firm's artist. His father, was particularly imbued with a spirit for fine design and realised the commercial value of having on his staff a competent artist/graphic designer whose skill might attract valuable business. On leaving the Central Secondary School, William worked for a year in the family firm learning the principles of the printing craft. He had been attending evening classes at the Sheffield School of Art since the age of eleven but then, at the age of fourteen, he became a full-time student for two years. At age of sixteen he joined the Sheffield Daily Telegraph as a trainee artist which enabled him to develop his skill in the techniques of drawing for the graphic reproduction processes. He remained there for three years during which time he not only continued studying part-time at the School of Arts and Crafts but also undertook some of the teaching. He achieved considerable success. He was awarded a National Gold Medal for Book Printing and Design and two Bronze Medals. In his final year at Sheffield he was awarded a Royal Exhibition Scholarship to the value of £60 which was tenable at the Royal College of Art, South Kensington. William after two years of study in the School of Design was awarded his Diploma and spent his final year in the School of Painting. He was now twenty-six years old and having become engaged, returned to Sheffield with a view to settling down and becoming an artist-designer-printer.

The career of the youngest son, Ernest, had taken a very different route. On leaving Ackworth School he had become a trainee pharmaceutical chemist. Finding the work to his liking he became qualified after studying at the Manchester School of Pharmacy. He returned to Sheffield and joined the then well-respected Sheffield pharmacy of G. T. W. Newsholme Limited. However, in 1910, Ernest, on joining the 3rd West Riding Field Ambulance Unit, had a become a member of the newly established Territorial Army, becoming, No. 173 Private E. Northend. By 1914, he had been promoted to the rank of Corporal and found himself, on the 4th August, in the throes of mobilisation.

Ernest Northend

The 'Call to Arms' following the Declaration of War immediately prompted Edgar, William and a number of members of Northend's staff to consider enlisting. J. W. Northend, already anticipating a shortage of staff immediately ruled that Edgar's place was necessary in the running of the business. Meanwhile, William Frederick presented himself for enlistment in the Sheffield City Battalion, which was subsequently to become the 12th 'Sheffield Pals' Battalion, York and Lancaster Regiment. William almost passed his medical examination but he failed the chest measurement requirement. The doctor who was examining him advised him to *'go home and swing a couple of Indian clubs about for a month and then come again'.* William went home discomfited, but when his brother Ernest, who was then serving in the 3rd West Riding Field Ambulance, heard of his misfortune advised him to *'come and join our mob,* they'll take anything'. Immediately, William went to the Field Ambulance Recruiting Centre, enlisted and, on 1st October, 1914, armed with a railway warrant and his acceptance papers, journeyed to Sandbeck Park, where he joined his brother Ernest in the Field Ambulance Unit. On 15th April, 1915, the unit was posted to France with 148 Brigade, forming part of the 49th West Riding Division. The two brothers served together, more or less, throughout the war.

All went well for Ernest Northend until September 1915. At this time, a number of members of the unit were promoted. It was then that Corporal Ernest, who felt he had been by-passed, took exception, relinquished his corporal's stripes and rejoined the ranks as a Private serving as a Stretcher-bearer until the end of the war. However, his service in the field was not without distinction. In 1916, he was decorated with the Military Medal for bravery when he went through heavy shell fire to rescue a wounded soldier during the opening battle of the Somme.

By the Summer of 1915, Edgar Thornton Northend felt increasingly isolated because he was not serving his country. His father, then aged fifty-nine was relying increasingly on him to keep the firm in business. The situation was to change. By the Summer of 1915, after fifteen months of war, it was becoming obvious that the flow of voluntary recruits could not be relied upon. Casualties, even in a quiet period, were occurring at the rate of 5,000 per week. However, both the Government and the War Office were reluctant to introduce conscription. Lord Derby, who had been an inspirational figure in recruiting volunteers, initiated a compromise. Every man between the ages of 19 and 42 was required to register. If he was not engaged in work of national importance or employed in war production, he could volunteer within six weeks and serve in a Regiment of his own choice or, wait six weeks and be called to the colours and sent to a unit where'er the Army chose. In view of this, Edgar volunteered for service with the Honourable Artillery Company on the 9th December 1915, but, being able to speak German, he was transferred to the Field Headquarters, Royal Engineers and put on intelligence interception work, picking up radio signals and translating them into English.

Meanwhile, William and Ernest, exercised their not inconsiderable talents. Whilst serving in France they established a unit magazine: 'The Lead Swinger' for the 3rd West Riding Field Ambulance Unit. Many have commented on the not too complimentary title, a title which implies shirking and scrounging. The reason lay in the British Army's attitude. Soldiers were in the Army to fight and win battles. Anyone engaged in noncombatant duties were considered to be scroungers. Traditionally, the only recognised ambulance facility and support when a battalion was in action was provided by the thirty-two or so regimental bandsmen, who were designated Stretcher-bearers. However, the casualty figures sustained in the Boer War began to change this attitude. The War Office, conscious of the inadequate arrangements for treating the wounded and sick when on Active Service, established the Royal Army Medical Corps in 1898. Following the horrendous casualty rate of the Somme offensive, 1st July 1916, the infantry battalions and the War Office both had good reason to thank the Royal Army Medical Corps and its associated Field Ambulance Units, whilst, the 3rd West Riding Field Ambulance basked in glory of 'The Lead Swinger' epithet.

It is interesting to compare the other and more widely known, trench journal, The Wiper's Times with The Lead Swinger. Typographically, the Wiper's Times was essentially a letterpress product. Typeset, using a variety of fonts and a whole array of typographical ornaments it was a remarkable achievement produced under battle conditions. In contrast, The Lead Swinger was a single manuscript tract which was passed around within the unit. It was essentially calligraphic and autographic in its layout and text. It reflects the work of 'Pipsqueak', the pen-name of Private Alfred Jackson, William Frederick Northend, and the Editor, Ernest Northend. Within the contents of the various issues, the fine penmanship and calligraphy of W. F. Northend is evident, so too are the highly stylised, black and white cartoons, evidence of the skill he acquired during his employment with the Sheffield Telegraph.

The remains of the Cathedral Porch at Arras in 1918,
sketched by William Northend

Both The Wiper's Times and The Lead Swinger, are journals which reflect the incredible spirit of those whose patriotism lead so many to untimely deaths or permanent incapacity. Many of those who did survive, seldom wished to discourse on their experiences. After the war, the various issues of The Lead Swinger were reprinted by the family firm: J. W. Northend Limited as a contribution to wartime memorabilia. A copy was lodged with the Imperial War Museum.

Roy Millington

Walter Terry

Walter Terry

Walter Terry was born on Christmas Eve 1895 to John and Patience Terry in Grimesthorpe, Sheffield. He was the youngest of nine children. He served his apprenticeship as a fettler and he went on to become a grinder. He enlisted in the Royal Army Medical Corps with the 3rd West Riding Field Ambulance and was stationed at Sandbeck Park, Maltby. Walter, known as Bob, volunteered for foreign service, along with his friends including his future brother-in-law, John Emmerson. Part of his time was spent in Grimsby from where he wrote to his mother *'having beautiful weather, getting along fine, should be better if I got a good bed'*.

Private Terry went to France and Flanders with his unit working in the trenches but despite what he saw he wrote to his sweetheart on May 26th, 1918, *'I am in the pink and in the best of spirits. We are having good weather'*. Whilst there, he was gassed but survived and married his sweetheart in 1920. That year, a baby girl was born and after that a son. However, Walter contracted pneumonia and died in May 1923. He is buried in Burngreave Cemetery. His daughter, Kathleen, remembers being given a penny to get a poppy on Armistice Day and pinning Walter's medals on her and her brother's chests, going to church where an army officer asked to whom the medals belonged. His widow fought to get a pension from the War Office as she believed her husband would have lived but for the gassing. The British Legion were involved somewhere along the way but a pension was not paid. Kathleen never bought a poppy after that, as the family suffered.

Pat Hall

My Grandfather, Private Walter Thwaites (1889-1963)

Walter Thwaites

Private Walter Thwaites was a horse despatch rider in the 2nd Battalion York and Lancs in Salonika, taking messages between H.Q. and the front lines. He was shot through the abdomen at waist level whilst acting as a decoy. His injury occurred in the winter of 1915-16 when snow was on the ground and he believed it was the cold that stopped the bleeding and saved his life; apparently no vital organ was touched. Fortunately he was found and taken to a casualty clearing station where his wounds were packed and they slowly healed. When he was well enough he was sent back to England to convalesce in Sheffield at Collegiate Hall (3rd NGH).

In civilian life before the War, Walter had been apprenticed to a 'Little Mester' and subsequently forged blades at his own hearth, he also boxed professionally. After the War he took up both these activities again but as the depression hit he did what work he could to provide for a growing family. During WW2 he undertook fire-watching. He died when I was seven years old, aged 74 years.

Denise Thwaites Bee

Shell Shock in World War One

Private Arthur Sweetingham, born in 1887, was awarded a Silver War Badge (otherwise known as a Discharge Badge or Wound Badge or Services Rendered Badge). He had volunteered in 1915 and been admitted to Wharncliffe War Hospital in Sheffield on October 23rd, 1916, ten days after an incident whilst carrying bombs as far as the communication trench. He was suffering from neurasthenia (nerves, headaches and disturbed sleep). He was discharged after 133 days and also discharged from the army – hence the Silver War Badge. This Badge was intended to be worn in the lapel of civilian clothing to demonstrate that the individual had 'done his bit' and to save him from the ignominy of being given a white feather.

Everyone has a mental picture of what 'shell shock' means but it was by no means clear what it was or how to deal with it during the First World War. Indeed some people with what appeared to be the same symptom complex had not been exposed to heavy shell fire and it was by no means unknown in the Air Arm of the services. Whilst nowadays it would probably be classified as Post Traumatic Stress Disorder (PTSD) it had many diagnostic labels attached to it during the First World War. The total number suffering from shell shock under the various names attached to it are unknown though figures of 80,000 are quoted and even then regarded as a conservative estimate! It is known that even 10 years after the war ended 25,000 men were still receiving a war pension because of the diagnosis. The British Army disapproved of the term and actually tried to ban it later, in part because of the implications it had for causation by war exposure rather than some pre-existing defect in the soldier himself and thus for the award of a wound stripe and allowances and pension rights. The term shell shock will be used in this account because it continues to represent the popular view of these men at that time.

This difficulty in knowing what to call it is exemplified by the diagnostic labels attached to soldiers admitted to Winter Street Hospital (later St George's Hospital) in Sheffield during the course of the war (see table). It is almost certain that all of these men suffered a variation on the same disorder.

Whilst shell shock accounts for around a quarter of the diagnostic labels this term was much more likely to be used earlier on in the course of the war rather than later. Neurasthenia, on the other hand, was a label very much more used towards the end of the War (41 of the 44) from December 1917 onwards. Nervous Debility, which may be interchangeable with Neurasthenia, also predominates towards the end of the War with 2 out of the 3 thus labelled coming after July 1917. The other terms are merely descriptive of the predominating symptom (Aphonia, Deaf and Dumb, Stammering, Loss of Memory) or are actually pejorative – Wilful Aphonia, Hysteria, Mental.

Diagnosis	Number
Shell Shock	34
Neurasthenia	44
Aphonia/Wilful Aphonia (1)/Loss of Speech	7
Hysteria	2
Dumb/Deaf and Dumb	4
Mental	2
Nervous Debility	3
Loss of Memory	1
Stammering	1

Records from Wharncliffe War Hospital are sparse but the Superintendent's reports to the Board show that a Mental Block opened in May 1917 with 20 beds. Initially there were only 3 patients but 22 are recorded by July 1917 and the figure throughout the rest of the war varied between these figures. Although there are no records available for the soldiers treated there the Superintendent's Report reveals an interesting insight into treatment by describing a man who had worked at the Asylum before the war and subsequently after going to fight had been discharged from the army as a result of shell shock. This man, named Tudsbury, was accepted back working at the Asylum in 1918. Various short extracts record him as being paid a wage at the establishment but also receiving treatment. He is recorded as not making much progress with his illness but the various treatments applied included massage and electrical therapy. One other ex-soldier named Waldron was engaged in December 1918 by the Asylum. He is said to have been 'broken down' by neurasthenia and was brought into the hospital as a patient for treatment with 'electric baths etc'.

Early in the war, it was felt that shell shock was probably due to some form of concussive brain injury following exposure to blast or perhaps a reaction to carbon monoxide poisoning from the fumes created by exploding armaments. Later the feeling grew that it was a reaction to exposure to the extreme stresses of war leading to a form of psychological breakdown. Certainly the illness was seen in people who had not been exposed to heavy bombardment or been in the vicinity of heavy fire. Some officers and doctors, however, continued to view it as cowardice or due to lack of moral fibre.

Dr. Charles Myers was perhaps the first to use the term shell shock in print (though he stressed he did not invent it) in case studies reported in the Lancet. He was commissioned in the RAMC. He took the view that shell shock was both a psychological and treatable condition but was frustrated that many did not agree with his views.

Dr. Aldren Turner, sent to France to investigate the problem reported that it was *'a form of temporary nervous breakdown scarcely justifying the name of neurasthenia, ascribed to a sudden or alarming psychical cause such as witnessing a ghastly sight or a harassing experience... the patient becomes 'nervy', unduly emotional and shaky, and most typical of all his sleep is disturbed by bad dreams... of experiences through which he has passed. Even the waking hours may be distressful from acute recollections of these events. Recovery is satisfactory, especially if the patient is sent home for complete rest'.*

The symptoms ranged from those that might then be described as neurasthenia– tiredness, headaches, confusion, inability to concentrate, nightmares, shaking – to those, fewer in number, that appeared similar to hysterical conversion – paralysis without overt neurological cause, aphonia, mutism, fugue and dramatic gait disturbances. Treatment ranged from physical to psychological. Dr. Lewis Yealland championed physical methods in London. He used massage and faradism to paralysed muscle groups. This could include increasingly strong faradic stimulation of the muscles of the throat in instances of mutism – a treatment that may appear barbaric by today's standards though not at the time. Whether this was similar to the electrical therapies referred to above at Wharncliffe War Hospital is difficult to know from the records available but was presumably at least a variation on it. Others, perhaps Dr W. H. R. Rivers at Craiglockhart War Hospital is amongst the best examples, employed predominantly psychological methods which might today be described as psychotherapy. Both these doctors firmly believed that their approach was the appropriate one in the circumstances in which they found themselves.

After the war, the War Office set up an enquiry into the nature of shell shock. It was prompted to do so for a number of reasons: not only did widely differing views on shell shock persist ranging from cowardice and malingering through to mental illness but there were also pressures to look into executions of soldiers during the war and whether they were actually suffering from shell shock. Additionally there were the post-war financial pressures of a worsening economy and pressures to reduce the war pensions budget – in 1920 there were 65,000 ex-servicemen receiving a pension for neurasthenia. The committee of enquiry took evidence from many doctors including Major W. J. Adie MD, MRCP, RAMC and Dr. William H. R. Rivers already mentioned above. A synopsis of their evidence to the committee is given below.

Major Adie, an Australian who had trained in medicine in Edinburgh, had joined the army as a doctor at the outbreak of war and had served throughout the war at the Western Front. After the war he worked as a civilian publishing on neurological matters and acted as a neurologist to the Ministry of Pensions. He described shell shock as any state of mind or body engendered or perpetuated by fear, which rendered a man less efficient in doing his duty or enabled him to avoid his duty altogether without punishment (his words). He felt that most soldiers suffered from a reduced efficiency in carrying out their duties but who, nevertheless, had continued to serve at the Front and to cope. His view was that those who broke down and left the Front were much more likely to come from units where the officers and doctors were of a poorer quality and he used the examples of the vastly differing numbers in two battalions serving side by side at the Front where he regarded the quality of the officers and doctors in the battalion with most cases of shell shock as being much inferior. He stated that the key to preventing, or at least much reducing, shell shock was in keeping up the morale of the troops by good leadership.

Dr. Rivers had worked at the Craiglockhart War Hospital for officers with shell shock or neurasthenia or similar diagnoses and later with air crew in the flying services. He preferred not to use the term shell shock but considered that the crucial factor was stress. He felt that any 'shock' was merely the final straw and might be related to a particularly unpleasant experience during shelling or any other especially unpleasant experience which might have nothing to do with shelling or gunfire. He contrasted men who broke down quickly with those who endured prolonged stressful experiences and finally collapsed after what might seem relatively trivial occurrences. He felt the former men were often poorly trained and were often not men of the regular army but those in it only for the duration of the war. He felt many of them had not wanted to be there and were stressed long before they reached the Front; they were, essentially, men unsuited to being soldiers at all. They felt little or no shame at suffering shell shock and often recovered quickly on being removed from the fighting. The more regular soldiers on the other hand tended to break down only after prolonged stresses (sleeplessness, anxiety, fatigue, responsibility – officers were more commonly diagnosed than other ranks), and when it happened, symptoms were often more severe and prolonged and harder to treat. They were also more likely to feel a sense of shame at having let down their comrades.

Whilst there is some common ground between these two opinions, it seems that Major Adie is more inclined to view some men as giving in to cowardice or outright malingering.

The committee reported on its findings in 1922 which included:
1. No soldier should be allowed to think that loss of nervous or mental control provides an honourable escape from the battlefield
2. If possible less severe cases should be treated with simple psychotherapy and be prevented from leaving the Front
3. Medical officers should be acquainted with the rudiments of psychology
4. Proper screening of recruits was essential
5. The term shell shock should be abolished
6. Shell shock cases should be treated separately from men with physical wounds
7. Unit morale and discipline are essential to prevention
8. Short tours of duty, frequent rotation and home leave are recommended

In view of the wide variation in opinion and the difficulty of distinguishing 'real' mental illness from malingering perhaps the final word should rest with Edward Casey who wrote a memoir called 'The misfit soldier' – an account of his 4 years at war and written long after the events. Edward Casey was a semi-illiterate soldier born in 1898 who enlisted in 1914. He felt himself a misfit and his record as a soldier was poor even before he reached the Front – he had deserted several times. He admits in the memoir to attempting to avoid duty by feigning madness. After heavy bombardment near Ypres, the worst he had experienced, he describes himself as having decided he 'had had enough'. He lay in the mud with his tunic over his head and was picked up by stretcher bearers and taken to a Casualty Clearing Station where he was diagnosed as suffering from shell shock and moved to a Base Hospital. He relates having *'the usual tests'* and answering *'I don't remember'* to everything. He was evacuated to Bristol and treatment included hypnosis. He felt certain they would discover he was malingering and he would be for the firing squad. Then during an air raid alert with anti-aircraft fire in the vicinity he decided the solution had come and he ran about shouting and said he was *'becoming expert at putting on a shivering fit'*. He was eventually told that he needed rest, exercise and good food and was thus able to avoid the war at least for a while.

Rodney Amos

The 3rd West Riding Field Ambulance in November 1915 probably at Estaires, near Lille, France.
- drawn by W. F. Northend

Joseph Ryle Clarke

In early May 1915 his body lay in the mortuary of a field dressing station near Ypres in western Belgium. Shot twice in the head, in his 20th year, he was gazetted as 'killed by enemy action'; the devastating news soon reaching his family and friends in Sheffield; and his passing was honoured by flags flown at half-mast over the University of Sheffield. Who was this young man who would rise from the dead to live a long, happy and successful life? What were the nature and circumstances of his injuries, and by what extraordinary constellation of circumstances did he come to survive and prosper? Joe Clarke's is an utterly remarkable and singularly Sheffield-centred story of chance, medical excellence, fortitude and deliverance.

Following his graduation (University of Sheffield; BSc Physics 1914) he had directly enlisted in the King's Own Yorkshire Light Infantry (KOYLI) as a volunteer in Haig's Expeditionary Army. He arrived in France in December 1915 as part of the regiment's Special Research Section and he was commissioned as a Lieutenant on 5th February 2015. The young officer was posted to the 2nd Battalion KOYLI which was deployed as part of the 13th Brigade of the 5th Division at the time he was shot. His Company's role on the front line was as part of the British defensive deployment

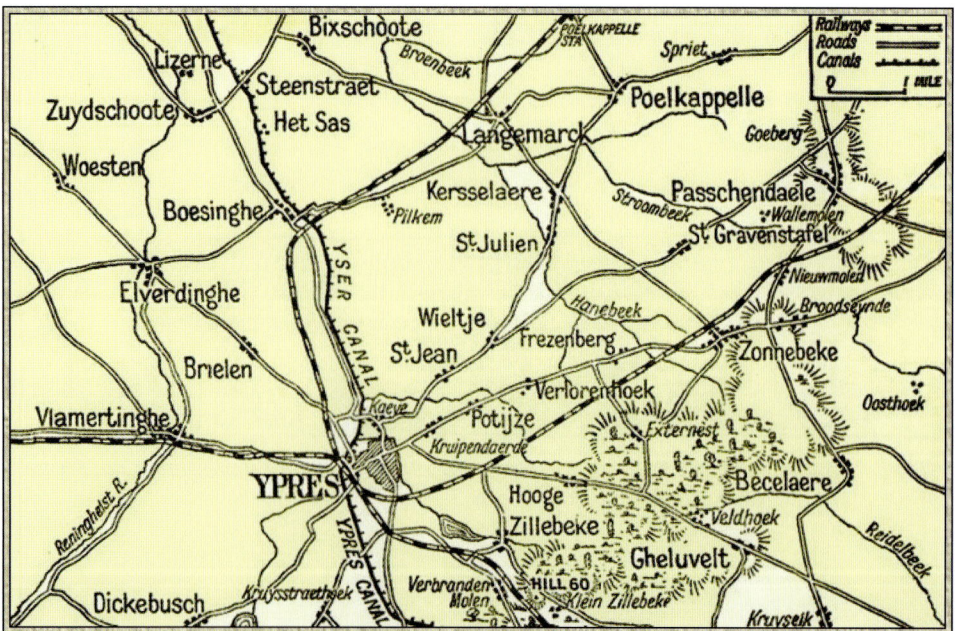

The Western Front at Ypres, Flanders

during a period in the 2nd Battle of Ypres which culminated in the German recapture of the notorious Hill 60 about three miles south-east of Ypres. Captured by the British in mid-April, using tactics that included the first use of the massive underground explosive mines that feature in Sebastian Faulks' novel 'Birdsong', Hill 60 was retaken by the German army over the 5th and 6th of May 1915 in action that was heavily influenced by gas attacks on the British trenches. Joe Clarke must have fully witnessed, if not experienced, all the manifold horrors of WW1 Infantry life on the Western Front. The geography and military dispositions in the area are well illustrated by the maps and sketches published in Arthur Conan Doyle's 'A History Of The Great War – Volume 2'.

During the night of the 7th/8th May 1915 Joe was struck, virtually simultaneously, twice in the head by bullets. The first became 'partially lodged' in his brain. The second, said to be a ricochet from sandbags, blew off part of his skull. He fell unconscious, was evacuated to a field dressing station, examined and certified as dead. His body was then removed to the adjacent mortuary, where we first encountered him, to await disposal by burial. Who knows how the story might then have played out? In reality his batman obtained permission to visit the corpse of the officer he served, surely an indication of the respect, standing and affection that Joe Clarke must have engendered over a relatively short period among the men he led. The batman lifted the white shroud to view his face and the movement of air is said to have induced a flutter of an eyelid. Clearly an observant fellow, he was greatly alarmed and rushed to inform the Colonel of the Regiment who repeated the observations. Lieutenant Clarke was alive but was deeply unconscious. He was summarily transferred to a hospital in Boulogne and his family rapidly received this amended, though still grave, news. His father urgently contacted Colonel Connell, military surgeon commanding the 3rd Northern General Hospital based in Sheffield. Colonel Connell agreed to arrange Joe's transfer back to his native city and surgically removed the bullet that had remained partially embedded in his brain.

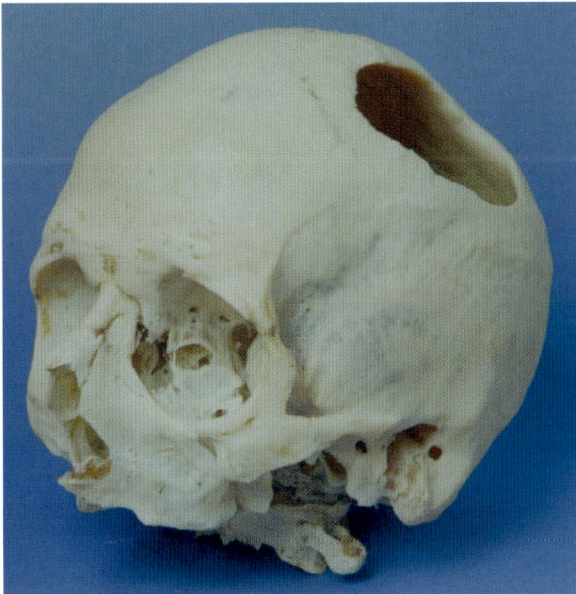

Joe Clarke's Skull

There remained the singular problem of the skull defect caused by the second bullet. This measured 8.5cm by 4cm situated close to the vertex, high on the left side of the head. The surgical closure of traumatic skull defects, cranioplasty, is considered to be an ancient part of medicine. The Incas are said to have used precious metals to fashion plates to close holes created by trepanation, and in the 16th Century there is a reference to the use of gold as a cranioplasty material in the writings of Fallopius. Readers of the naval Aubrey/Maturin novels of Patrick O'Brian will be very familiar with the episode where Dr Maturin 'rouses the Gunner's brains' by treating a depressed skull fracture at sea, caused by falling rigging. The successful operation, using a metal disc fashioned from a coin and all witnessed on deck by the ship's crew, lastingly elevates the Good Doctor's standing. However, even in the early part of the 20th century, cranioplasty remained an obscure and rarely utilised operation. Undoubtedly the massive upsurge in head injuries sustained by soldiers on all sides during WW1 was one of the stimuli that drove the major advances in the practice and development of cranioplasty techniques and materials that characterise modern neurosurgery. Colonel Connell made the fateful decision to undertake cranioplasty and performed the operation in Sheffield in September 1915. A gold plate was commissioned from Mappin and Webb using gold of 98.4% purity. The plate was made with a serrated edge and with peripheral holes around the rim to enable the growth of fibrous tissue during healing to ultimately stabilise its position over the skull defect. Measuring 15cm by 11cm it weighed 135g so that its present day scrap bullion value amounts to more than £3,500. A new one today might cost more than £6,000. The operation was entirely successful and his ultimate recovery remarkable.

Gold Cranioplasty Plate

The many contemporaneous and subsequent accounts of Joe Clarke's life indicate that he was spared the seriously debilitating long-term complications that arise as sequelae of major head trauma and brain injury (e.g. epilepsy, cognitive and behavioural changes). This was a surgical success of the first order. Initially he did sustain a right-sided hemiplegia (examination of the skull defect suggests that the left primary motor cortex was likely to have been affected by his injury) but subsequent accounts suggest a good neurological outcome over a recovery period of several years. His major residual deficit was unilateral hearing loss. Historical accounts of his life refer to a necessity to undergo other operative procedures over a number of years. Joe himself was sufficiently motivated by the skill of the medical care he received that he requested in his Will that his skull, and the cranioplasty plate, be retained by the Pathology Department of the University of Sheffield in perpetuity for medical and public education; *'To be an inspiration to future medical students'*. As a consequence the photographs accompanying this account are of the actual skull and the gold plate as removed and prepared for display in the Professor W. A. J. Crane Museum of Pathology at the time of Joe Clarke's death in 1983.

Before leaving this remarkable medical history further footnotes need to be mentioned. He suffered full hearing loss in the left ear and partial loss in the right. This was investigated and improved by the Sheffield Ear Surgeon John Gray FRCS who performed a novel and successful procedure to bypass the ossicles within the middle ear. In 1975 he sustained a fall resulting in bilateral mandibular fractures and a broken nose. The jaw fractures were treated surgically using Vitallium (an alloy of 60% cobalt, 20% chromium, 5% molybdenum) plate and wire.

What then was the life of this remarkable survivor of the arbitrariness of fate awaiting all who were deployed to the frontline trenches of Flanders in early 1915? The drama of his enlistment, injury, survival and restoration to health are matched by the length and richness of his subsequent life. Upon his recovery he returned to his academic studies and graduated MSc in Physics in 1917. He remained an enlisted officer on Home duty until the end of the war when he was discharged from the army with the rank of Captain. Both as an undergraduate and following his injury he enjoyed a highly supportive and friendly relationship with Professor Hicks and his successor Professor Milner in the Department of Physics at Sheffield University. From 1917 until the end of the war, at Prof Hick's recommendation he was seconded to the Ministry of Munitions to work in the University's Glass Department, under Professor W. E. R. Turner, on spectroscopy. He then pursued a diverse early career. From 1919 at the London Radium Centre he was preparing radium applicators and radium tubes for therapeutic applications. He also was involved in assessing issues around the health and safety of nurses and other staff who worked with radioactive materials. He was appointed in 1920 as the first physicist employed in the Metropolitan-Vickers company at Trafford Park to act as the Chief of a new research department. In 1921, Professor Milner offered him an Assistant Lectureship back in his old Department in Sheffield which he accepted as the base for the remainder of his working life. He published scientific papers on radiology, spectroscopy and electricity and translated a number of works from French to English. Among his many roles and achievements, acknowledged by his promotion to Lecturer and then Senior Lecturer, was his involvement as physics tutor to the undergraduate 1st MB ChB course, then an obligatory component of the pre-clinical medical course, so that there are warm accounts of his dedication to Sheffield's aspiring doctors and of the regard and affection in which he was held by the student body. He was also highly active in support of student sporting events. He was elected an honorary member of the Medical Old Students Association, the only non-medic to be so honoured.

During WW2 he again volunteered his services which were readily accepted. His work on this occasion involved the supervision of a de-Gaussing campaign to reduce the threat of German magnetic mines to Allied shipping. He was primarily deployed in this role in the Port of London and then at Scapa Flow in the Orkneys to protect the Royal Navy's Grand Fleet. He loved to tell the tale of how in London, dressed in his University of Sheffield blazer, he first called in at the Port Admiral's office to report for duty. Announced into the office the Admiral was expecting to receive a salute from this Captain Clarke dressed in naval uniform. The University blazer however quite phased the Admiral who thus rose himself to salute the totally unfamiliar uniform before him. This admiralty work completed he returned to Sheffield and joined the Sheffield University Officer Training Corps for the remainder of the War.

Joe Clarke in later life

Joe Clarke retired from the University in 1954 due to the breakdown of his health at the age of 60 years. However for the next 30 years he remained very active in two spheres of particular interest to him, the Church and Freemasonry. His Church activities included the role of Church Warden in Hathersage, and as a member of the Diocesan Council of Education. Within the Masons he was highly active as a researcher, delivering the Prestonian Lecture to the Grand Lodge of England in 1969. He was subsequently invited to contribute the major part of a history of the Grand Lodge published in commemoration of the 250th anniversary of its founding. An associated paper accepted for publication on the Regius Manuscript of 1390AD had required him to master Early (Chaucerian) English.

Joe Clarke married Constance Muirhead in 1922 who sadly died in childbirth in 1926. His daughter, Dorothy Muriel Clarke (McCann) survived him. He remarried in 1929 to Dorothy Muirhead, the sister of his first wife, and they shared 46 fulfilling years of marriage together. Ultimately her health failed and she passed away leaving Joe a widower for the second time. Shortly after this, his great friend the ear surgeon John Gray also died widowing his wife Ursula. They had been very close in friendship as married couples and Joe's many friends were delighted when he and Ursula decided to enter a marriage which lasted happily until his death on 1st February 1983 at the age of 89 years.

In postscript it is appropriate to add a few comments about the career of Arthur M. Connell ChM FRCS (Ed), the surgeon who treated Joe Clarke's head injuries during WW1. The life of Colonel Connell is recounted by his grandson, Miles Connell elsewhere in this book. A gifted surgeon and distinguished teacher, the legacy of his work as a military surgeon in WW1 will live on through the remarkable story that is the death and life of J. R. Clarke.

Paul Ince

A patient's view
– experiences of a casualty

My father, Lt. William Fred Fletcher, was shot down over France on 22nd April 1917 whilst returning from a photo-reconnaissance mission, thus becoming the Red Baron's 46th victim. He had joined the Royal Flying Corps (RFC) from the Machine Gun Corps, we think in 1916 – his records have been lost from the National Archives so what follows is culled from various sources, some anecdotal. In spite of collecting 11 lead bullets in his right arm plus an explosive one near his right foot he managed

William Fletcher having ditched after his first solo flight

to land his Fe2b on our side of the lines, where, according to the official crash report, it cart-wheeled head-over-heels twice before coming to rest. Somehow both he and his observer, Lt. Franklin, survived.

After first-aid treatment in the field, Dad was transferred back through the casualty clearing system, eventually reaching the hospital at Boulogne where his right arm was amputated about three inches below the shoulder. My mother always said that the operation was not very well performed, leaving a very ragged stump, but Dad was only too happy to have survived. His right foot, which was semi-protected by his own personal thick fur lined boots, escaped with only minor injuries although it remained sensitive for the rest of his life. After recovery, Dad was repatriated to a convalescent centre near Windsor, re-joining the RFC as an instructor at RFC Uxbridge until demobilisation, when he resumed his engineering studies as a graduate apprentice at Turner Newalls in Coventry.

We don't know when he moved to Sheffield. What we do know is that sometime in the mid-1920s, at Ashover, a village south of Chesterfield, he met my mum, Doris Butler, a local girl and a medical student at Sheffield University. They married after her graduation in March 1930 and set up home, first in Whitely Lane, and secondly, on the edge of the moors in Townhead Road, Dore. In 1936, he caught tuberculosis and was hospitalised at the Edward VII hospital in Midhurst. (It is rumoured that I was conceived in the hospital grounds in the back of their Austin 7; having owned an Austin 7, I find this story hard to believe!) On recovery, he joined the Ministry of Supply as Assistant Controller E & W Riding, rising to Controller in 1948, one of the first engineers to be promoted into an administrative position. After another bout of tuberculosis in 1948, surviving only thanks to the new antibiotic, streptomycin, in 1954 he retired from the Ministry, working as a consulting engineer until his death on 29th Dec 1961, aged 67 yrs.

Dad spoke very little of his wartime experiences but we think he must have taken some time to adjust to his disability. However, as a true engineer, he rose to the challenge and taught himself to be left handed. Whilst in Coventry, getting fed up with commuting in the rain, he adapted his motorbike to be driven from the sidecar; it is probably apocryphal but he claimed that, with his fellow student sitting backwards on the pillion reading a newspaper, he got past four traffic policemen before being stopped. As long as the gearstick and handbrake were on the left hand side, he could drive any car and became one of the earliest disabled members of the Institute of Advanced Motoring. He had a variety of gadgets that he fixed to his artificial arm, enabling him to complete any number of household, gardening and DIY tasks, to ride a bicycle and to continue his carpentry hobby. The baby's crib he made for his first born is still in the family, now awaiting his great-great grandchildren.

Until the second bout of TB, he was fit and active, playing tennis and walking the paths and hills of the local area. After 1948, almost any exercise was a strain and just walking up stairs was a major effort. In spite of this he continued to be as active as he could, went gliding at Hucknall, came sailing with me in a 12 ft dinghy and taught himself how to handle a small motor cruiser on the Norfolk Broads. But perhaps the greatest problem from his RFC service was his deafness. Spending months just inches from a high powered aero engine caused severe noise-induced high-frequency deafness later in his life and by the end of the World War II, he had been forced to wear a hearing aid. Hearing aids in those days were not the tiny in ear devices you get today but were the size of a pack of playing cards, clipped to one's jacket lapel and hardwired to the battery pack round the waist and to the ear pieces. Nothing daunted, he went stereophonic with a second unit, greatly enhancing the benefit to his hearing if not to the overall sartorial effect.

My mum, Dr. Doris Fletcher (nee Butler) spent almost the whole of her working career as a Consultant Dermatologist in the Sheffield area. After retirement, she moved to Wiltshire and, practised virtually to the end, dying of cancer on 21st March, 1979.

Giles Fletcher

Archibald Cuff

Archibald William Cuff

One of the many prominent Sheffield doctors during WW1 was Archibald William Cuff. Born on 10th February, 1861 at The Swan Hotel, Rostherne, Cheshire, he was educated at Bowdon College before being admitted to St. John's College, Cambridge in 1888. He gained his BA in the Natural Science Tripos in 1891, completing his medical training at St. Thomas's Hospital, London gaining his MRCS and LRCP in 1893.

In 1895 he was appointed house physician to Sheffield Royal Infirmary where he met a young nurse, Harriet Cockbaine, who he married on 7th February 1900. During the next 25 years at the Royal Infirmary he helped lay the foundation of modern abdominal surgery and, on his retirement, was elected to the board of management. He was for some years lecturer in surgery at the University of Sheffield and an examiner in surgery for the University of Cambridge. From 1898 he had been medical referee for the Sheffield and Rotherham County Court Districts under the Workmen's Compensation Act.

Archibald Cuff received his commission as Surgeon-Lieutenant in the 4th West Riding of Yorkshire Volunteer Artillery in the sixty-third year of the reign of Queen Victoria on 4th May 1900. At the outbreak of war in August 1914 he received his call up notice requiring him to attend at the headquarters of 3rd West Riding Brigade, Royal Field Artillery no later than 10am on 5th August. On 8th September he was promoted to Surgeon-Major and served as medical officer with the Royal Field Artillery on the Western Front for the duration of the war, once being mentioned in despatches. Due to the shortage of bandages, he pioneered the use of sphagnum moss to treat wounds and a sizeable industry grew up on the Yorkshire moors. A few years after his return to civilian life he was appointed a Justice of the Peace.

At his funeral in 1938 the Bishop of Sheffield wrote, *'He was one of those men who gave their services voluntarily for the benefit of the less fortunate of our people, a splendid example of the noble profession of healing'*.

Rory Herbert

Reg's War

Reg or Waide Reginald Worrall was born in Sheffield in 1895 and volunteered to join up in August 1914 only a few days after the war was declared. He was assigned to the RAMC at Norfolk Barracks where he was based for training until 15th April 1915 although he spent some time at Gainsborough almost certainly at the John Coupland Hospital. He would have been 19 years old at the time. He arrived in France with the 3rd WRFA in April, 1915, a week before the second battle of Ypres and set up their field headquarters a little behind the front line at Estaires ready to receive casualties. He was in the bearer division of the field ambulance.

The camp at Estaires. Reg is at far right

Soldiers were forbidden to have cameras on the Western Front in order to maintain morale at home. Reg however, sent home a series of postcards from the front which vividly show the carnage of the battlefield and its effects on the neighbouring towns and villages. The most dramatic of these shows the burnt out ruins of the bell tower of the Mediaeval Cloth Hall at Ypres after the German bombardment in 1915. One postcard is written in a very shaky hand and reads *'Dear Mother, Excuse me not writing as I am working almost night and day and that is nearly all at the trenches'*. He was clearly involved in major battles, one series of postcards being sent in the aftermath of the battle of Loos and shortly after this he was gassed and admitted to his own field hospital. As a result of this he was granted 8 days home leave.

On returning to active service in February 1916 he sent a new series of postcards from around the Somme area, one of which says to his mother *'The place we are at now is very poor and we can't buy what we want so I could do with a parcel of grub now, if you care to send it'.* July 1st, 1916, was the opening day of the Battle of Albert, which became known as the Battle of the Somme and is remembered as the bloodiest day in the history of the British Army in which there were 57,470 casualties of whom 19,240 were killed or died of wounds. Lines of infantry were mown down by German machine guns and it took stretcher bearers and the ambulance corps a week to clear the wounded from the trenches and no man's land. Reg was almost certainly one of these stretcher bearers, his postcard home again written in a shaky hand, his only comment being that he had had a tottering time.

Exterieur de l'Hôtel-de-Ville et du Beffroi
1914... IN BELGIUM - YPRES
Exterior of the town hall and Belfrey

Ruins of the Mediaeval Cloth Hall, Ypres

Reg stayed in the trenches until February 1917 when he was identified as a candidate for officer training and promoted to lance corporal. He returned to England and completed his officer training successfully in November 1917 becoming a second lieutenant in the West Yorkshire Regiment. He returned to France in April 1918 being posted to a Trench Mortar Battery close to Craonne but was captured by the Germans on the first day of the Battle of the Aisne, also being badly wounded. He was treated in a German hospital and then transferred to the Karlsruhe 1B POW camp where he remained until a month after the Armistice.

Derek Cullen

I would like to thank Peter Rhodes, Reg's grandson, for his detailed research and preservation of family documents, photographs and postcards which have provided so much information about the 3rd West Riding Field Ambulance and the men who served in it.

Blood Transfusion in the Great War

It was during World War I that blood transfusion emerged as a life-saving medical treatment. This is a story of scientific and technical advances, circumstances, courage and luck.

Although there are accounts of blood transfusion prior to WWI it required numerous scientific and technical developments before transfusion became a practical reality. Briefly these were Landsteiner's discovery of ABO blood groups in 1900 (work for which he eventually received the Nobel Prize in 1930): Alexis Carrel's (a French surgeon, working in Canada) development of a technique of anastomosing arteries to veins; George Washington Crile's invention of a cannula which enabled blood to flow from one person's artery into another person's vein and Richard Lewisham's development of a non toxic solution of sodium citrate that prevented blood from clotting.

The courageous pioneers who brought blood transfusion into use during the war were Major Lawrence Bruce Robertson, a Canadian surgeon, and Oswald Hope Robertson, a US Army Captain.

Lawrence Bruce Robertson

L. B. Robertson graduated in medicine from the University of Toronto in 1909. He had learnt the syringe technique of transfusion (whereby measured volumes of blood are collected from a donor and then rapidly transfused into a recipient before the exposure to air could activate the clotting process) from Lindeman at Belleview Hospital Toronto and had described 27 such transfusions to children. At the time knowledge of typing techniques was not widespread.

At the outbreak of war in 1914 Robertson volunteered for service and was commissioned in the Canadian Army Medical Corps. He was shipped to England and thence to France in early 1915, where he was seconded to a British Base Hospital. At the time blood transfusion was viewed with disdain by the British medical establishment who saw 'no good reasons for abandoning the safe and simple method of saline injection'. Regardless of this Robertson performed four transfusions and described these in the British Medical Journal in June 1916. This was the first article on wartime blood transfusion in the 20th century.

In Feb 1916 he built a resuscitation ward at the Second Casualty Clearing ward and reported a series of 36 resuscitation transfusions, including three fatal transfusion reactions. It was at this stage that Gordon Watson, Consultant Surgeon to the British

Expeditionary Force declared that the British Army Medical Corp's conversion to transfusion was 'sudden and complete'.

The US entered World War I in April 1917 and with it came Dr. Oswald Hope Robertson.

Oswald Hope Robertson

O. H. Robertson graduated from the University of California in 1910. He carried out research in the laboratories of Roger Lee and Beth Vincent who had been to the American Volunteer Hospital in Paris and there performed the first recorded transfusion of the war on 23rd April, 1915. Robertson worked at the Rockefeller Institute on blood typing and red cell storage. In 1917 he joined the Harvard Medical Unit, a group committed to blood typing.

In May, 1917, the Harvard Medical Unit sailed to England where they spent two weeks and then moved to France directly behind the line in Flanders. By July, Dr. Roger Lee (in charge of the Harvard Medical Unit) had set up a system of identifying potential blood donors and posting their names and blood types on operating room doors and Robertson had developed a transfusion bottle using a solution of sodium citrate and glucose.

Sir George Makin, General of the British Expeditionary Force, asked R. Lee to look into the then British practice of using un-crossmatched blood as he was worried by the reported deaths. Robertson was sent to the British Third Army to demonstrate the use of universal stored blood. By December, 1917, the safety of using typed, syphilis tested, stored blood had been widely demonstrated.

It is a fitting tribute to end this brief account by quoting Sir Geoffrey Keynes, the eminent British surgeon who describes his wartime experiences in his book 'The Gates of Memory'.

'The Moribund Ward… contained all the patients regarded by a responsible officer as being probably past surgical aid, since it was our duty to operate where there was a reasonable hope of recovery rather than waste effort where there seemed to be none. The possibility of blood transfusion now raised hopes where formerly there had not been any , and I made it my business during any lull in the work to steal into the moribund ward, choose a patient who was still breathing and had a perceptible pulse, transfuse him and carry out the necessary operation. Most of them were suffering primarily from shock and loss of blood, in this way I had the satisfaction of pulling many men back from the jaws of death'.

Virge James

Charles Cecil Wildman Mays

Memorial to Dr. Charles Mays
- by kind permission of
St. Thomas's Church, Crookes, Sheffield

Charles Cecil Wildman Mays was born in Sheffield in 1878. He qualified as a doctor from Sheffield Medical School and entered general practice in the Crookes area of the city. He spent most of the war as a practitioner in Sheffield but in 1917 at the age of 40, he made the decision to join the RAMC and serve in France. Despite his age and experience, his rank when posted overseas in May 1917 was that of a lowly lieutenant. Unfortunately on the 25th July, 1918, he tragically lost his life when the transport ship 'Normandy' on which he was returning to France from England, presumably after a spell of leave, was torpedoed by a U-boat off the Cherbourg Peninsula. So within a year of taking that fateful decision to enlist in the prime of life, he was dead. He is commemorated on a memorial in the military section of the Sainte Marie Cemetery, Le Havre, as well as on a stained glass window erected to his memory in St. Thomas's Church, Crookes which refers to him as 'For Thirteen Years a Surgeon in this Parish'.

David Baldwin

John Ainley Bagshaw

John Ainley Bagshaw was born in 1894 and became a pupil at the King Edward VII Grammar School, Sheffield. The family business was etching trademarks and designs on flatware and tools from premises in Eyre Street. The traditional career route then was for sons to enter the family business. However, on completion of his education John Bagshaw, usually known as Jack, was sent by his father to Villach in Austria to study the German language. Jack's wish to study medicine was not considered appropriate, so on his return, he began work in the family business, James Bagshaw Ltd. Following the outbreak of war, he volunteered for service in the 3rd West Riding Field Ambulance and embarked for France in 1915.

John Bagshaw

As a stretcher-bearer and medical orderly, he saw many casualties and his daughter, Mrs Judith Dakin, relates how he used to say that he could tell whether a casualty was alive or dead by the displacement of the feet. Jack frequently worked with Ernest Finch and on one occasion, Finch leant over the operating table and, referring to Jack's somewhat prominent nose, said to him: *'I could straighten that thing for you'*. The offer was not accepted. Following his discharge from the Army, Jack returned to work in the family business. His dream of becoming a doctor went unfulfilled.

Roy Millington

Sister Margaret Ruth Fieldhouse

Margaret Ruth Fieldhouse in 1916

My mother, Margaret Ruth Fieldhouse was born in Rotherham in 1893, the youngest child of John William Fieldhouse, a boot and shoe factor, and his wife Harriet. John died when Ruth was a few days old. She was educated as a boarder at Notre Dame Convent High School, Liverpool, by the Notre Dame Sisters who were pioneers in women's education. The Goosens sisters, Sidonie and Marie, the well known harpists were day girls there and their father Eugene Goosens, the conductor and composer, used to give the students memorable lectures. Ruth had a life-long love of poetry and could recite a huge amount from memory, a gift many an actor would have envied.

She started her nursing training at the City of Coventry Isolation hospital gaining her certificate of training in 1911 but could not do general nursing training until she was 19 years old. She qualified from Manchester Royal Infirmary in medical and surgical nursing in 1917 and immediately joined the Territorial Nursing Force working throughout the war at Shiregreen School, Sheffield which had been taken over by the 3rd Northern General Hospital. Mother would sometimes share a few memories of her time nursing in Sheffield with me. She hated the sound of marching feet as it reminded her of the soldiers who came with frost bitten gangrenous toes hanging by a thread. There were numerous fractured femurs and amputations where not infrequently the stitches would break and the stump would be fountaining blood and she had to grab the artery with a pair of Spencer Wells forceps. On one occasion a mobile X-ray machine burst into flames and set fire to a soldier's dressing. He panicked and ripping off burning cotton wool from his knee and throwing it to either side he set fire to adjoining beds which mother extinguished with a blanket. There must have been cases of Spanish Flu at my mother's hospital as she said that *'people just turned blue and died very quickly'*.

I can never forget a young Welsh soldier of sixteen who had lied about his age who told mother that after he was wounded he came to in a shell hole and there was a German boy of about the same age. He said they shared a canteen of water and then put their arms round each other and *'We cried. And don't you tell a soul'*. At the end of the war there was a Victory Party. The centre piece was a big cake, a cross between a wedding cake and a war memorial. It was several tiers high, with figures of soldiers at the four corners and a winged victory on top – the whole decorated with lilies of the valley.

The Victory Cake

My mother met her future husband at Shiregreen Hospital when he came to her with his left hand bandaged asking if she could do anything with it as he played the fiddle. He explained that he had caught his hand in a bread slicing machine and cut off the tip of his forefinger which he produced in a clean handkerchief. Mother cleaned and dressed his finger and stuck the tip back onto the finger with collodion. It healed by first intention and Ruth married the soldier, Archibald Wilson Young, after the war in 1920 and they moved to Woking where I, their only child, still live.

Mary Wilson Young